The perfect book for today's rock fan, *The Story of Rock 'n' Roll* is a unique exploration of one of the most powerful cultural forces of our time.

With characteristic insight, veteran radio personality and rock historian Pete Fornatale chronicles the major developments in rock music, while discussing the artists, the social climate, and the radio and recording industries that helped shape the trends.

Along the way, you'll meet all the rock 'n' roll greats of the past and present—from fifties innovators Chuck Berry, Little Richard, and the "King," Elvis Presley...to the legendary Beatles and the British Invasion...to Bob Dylan and the roots of folk rock...to late sixties psychedelic rock, the San Francisco Sound, Jimi Hendrix, and the Doors...and on to Led Zeppelin and the explosion of heavy metal, ornately orchestrated progressive rock and the backlash of punk and New Wave in the seventies... right up to the "Boss," Bruce Springsteen, and the advent of MTV.

Filled with over fifty exciting photos, *The Story of Rock 'n' Roll* is a fascinating look at the music that has transformed our popular culture.

Pete Fornatale has been a radio personality at WNEW-FM, New York, since 1969. He is currently the host of "Saturday Morning Sixties" and "Mixed Bag," which won the 1983 Armstrong Award for Excellence in Broadcasting. The author of *The Rock Music Source Book* and *Radio in the Television Age,* he is also the creator and narrator of the nationally syndicated feature "Rock Calendar." While a student at Fordham University, he originated a progressive rock show there that was a forerunner of the FM format of the late sixties.

A former high school teacher, Fornatale lectures at various colleges. He lives in Port Washington, New York, with his wife and three sons.

Jacket photograph © 1987 Bob Gruen/Star File

William Morrow and Company, Inc.
105 Madison Avenue
New York, NY 10016

REINFORCED EDITION

L

THE STORY OF
ROCK
—'N'—
ROLL

THE STORY OF
ROCK
—'N'—
ROLL

PETE FORNATALE

FOREWORD BY GRAHAM NASH

WILLIAM MORROW AND COMPANY INC. NEW YORK

PHOTO CREDITS

Permission for photograph and picture reprint is gratefully acknowledged :

Michael Ochs Archives of Venice, California : pp. 4, 11, 13, 16, 18, 23, 25, 27, 31, 37, 40, 43, 44, 47, 58, 62, 63, 65, 71, 74, 78, 80, 85, 91, 94, 97, 105, 111, 116, 121, 127, 136, 145, 148, 150, 153, 155, 159, 160, 180.

Star File Photo Agency, Inc., of New York, New York : p. 21 (Pictorial Press), p. 102 (Bill Levy/Marquee), p. 108 (Lucas), p. 119 (Elliott Landy), p. 124 (Lucas), p. 141 (Kate Simon), p. 168 (Chuck Pulin), p. 171 (Chuck Pulin), p. 174 (Janet Macoska), p. 193 (Capak).

UPI/Bettman, Bettman Newsphotos, The Bettman Archive of New York, New York : p. 72.

The publisher and author would like to thank the copyright holders for permission to reprint lyrics from the following songs :

p. 8 : "Rock and Roll Is Here to Stay" by David White, © 1958, 1985 by David White.

p. 22 : "School Day" by Chuck Berry, copyright Isalee Music Company, Wentzville, Missouri.

p. 131 : "Woodstock" by Joni Mitchell, © 1969 by Siquomb Publishing Corp.

p. 191 : "Truckin'" by Jerome Garcia, Robert Weir, Philip Lesh, and Robert Hunter, © 1971 by Ice Nine Publishing Company, Inc.

Library of Congress Cataloging-in-Publication Data
Fornatale, Peter.
The story of rock 'n' roll.
Bibliography .
Includes index.
Summary : Traces the history of rock and roll music from
the 1950's to the present day and discusses its changing
styles and leading personalities.
I. Title.
ML3534.F68   1987   784.5'4'009   86-28453
ISBN 0-688-06276-8
ISBN 0-688-06277-6 (pbk.)

For Susan

ACKNOWLEDGMENTS

I'd like to begin by thanking my editor, Cathy Petrone, for giving me the opportunity to do this project in the first place. Her insights were uniformly excellent, and her suggestions were welcome at each stage of the process.

I'd also like to thank my friend and writing partner Alan Katz for his contributions to the manuscript. His unfailing generosity and good humor added immeasurably to my enjoyment of doing this book.

Thanks to Graham Nash for his insights and his music.

Thanks to Michael Ochs and Star File for their great archives.

And, finally, thanks to Peter, Mark, and Steven Fornatale for making me realize how essential it is to communicate a sense of importance about the things we love to the people we love ... and that certainly applies to rock 'n' roll!

FOREWORD

In England in the mid-fifties, over the ever-fading airwaves of Radio Luxembourg, I used to listen every Sunday night to records from the American Top Forty. As I quickly tired of the crooners and singers of white buckskin rock, it suddenly hit me. I was introduced to the driving force of Elvis, Little Richard, Jerry Lee Lewis, Fats Domino, Buddy Holly, Gene Vincent, and the Everly Brothers.

From the first moment that I heard the opening bars of "Bye, Bye, Love," I was truly overwhelmed by the need to affect people the same way that this record affected me. There was something incredibly raw, raucous, and audacious about this new form of self-expression in music, something that woke me up and shook me to the core. I can honestly say that I was never quite the same after hearing these great records.

I'd been singing folk and skiffle music since the early fifties, and it gave me a chance to practice the sense of harmony that my friend Allan Clarke and I had discovered on the school playground. Allan and I later formed the Hollies and started what was to become, hopefully, a lifetime contribution to the art of rock 'n' roll. Then in the late sixties, my dear friend, the late Cass Elliot of the Mamas and Papas, introduced me to David Crosby and consequently to Stephen Stills and Neil Young. By this time I was firmly dedicated to the idea that music could change minds and spirits for the better. It certainly changed mine.

One of the best things about *The Story of Rock 'n' Roll* is that it establishes the history of rock 'n' roll music and thereby gives us a brief glimpse of its effect on the lives of young people as they struggled with growing up. So many of the stories told here parallel my own, dreaming the dream, pulling toward the dream, and finally attaining it. All of the people profiled here created warm feelings and great memories. Pete Fornatale writes about them with obvious care and affection. Their stories come to life in the pages of this book.

The Story of Rock 'n' Roll is a book for rock fans of all ages, but I think it has particular value for young readers. It is a perfect introduction to the revolutionary music that changed the world.

Finally, the debt of gratitude I owe to the pioneers of rock 'n' roll can never be repaid, except by continuing to sing, write, and play my best, and perhaps inspiring other kids as I was inspired.

Long live rock 'n' roll!

CONTENTS

THE STORY OF ROCK 'N' ROLL

INTRODUCTION

On the evening of January 28, 1985, a group of musicians and singers began gathering at the main recording studio of A&M Records in Hollywood, California. It is common for such studios to be in use at all hours of the day or night all over the country for various purposes: jingles, commercials, albums, soundtracks, etc. But make no mistake about it, this was no ordinary group. They straggled in one at a time or in small combinations until the individuals in that room represented the single greatest gathering of pop musicians in one place at one time in the history of recorded music. Among them: Ray Charles, Harry Belafonte, Willie Nelson, Tina Turner, Bob Dylan, Paul Simon, Diana Ross, Michael Jackson, Kenny Rogers, Stevie Wonder, Billy Joel, Cyndi Lauper, Lionel Richie, and Bruce Springsteen.

It was the session for "We Are the World" by U.S.A. for Africa.

The greatest stars in the firmament of American popular music came together to record a song to aid the starving population of Ethiopia. It was a phenomenal gesture. Musicians had lent their talents to worthy causes before (notable among them: George Harrison's Concert for Bangladesh in 1971, the Save the Children Concert at the U.N. in 1979, and the ARMS Benefit in 1983), but never on the scale or magnitude of that memorable January night.

The occasion was noteworthy for many reasons, certainly the fund-raising and the consciousness-raising foremost among them. But above and beyond all that, it was noteworthy for its eloquent reminder of the sheer power and beauty of music as a universal communicator. Every conceivable ingredient that comprises the melting pot of American popular music was represented in that room—rhythm and blues, country and western, gospel, jazz, folk, and of course, rock 'n' roll.

How fitting! Rock 'n' roll, which for years had struggled to achieve acknowledgment and recognition in our culture, standing side by side, shoulder to shoulder, with every category of music to which it owes its very existence.

It certainly didn't start out that way. From the very beginning, rock 'n' roll has had to fight and claw and scratch its way toward acceptance. So even this recent progress is a little misleading, because there are still those who would blame many of the problems of youth on rock 'n' roll. And there probably always will be. Witness the 1985 congressional hearings about rating rock lyrics for listener safety and parental comprehension. Even some of those who grew up on rock seem not to understand what it is all about today. Rock 'n' roll continues to be a scapegoat for all kinds of complaints and misunderstandings. So the journey to acceptance is by no means over. And that's probably a good thing, too. After all, two of rock's primary functions have always been to annoy adults and to take a poke at the status quo.

This is precisely how it must be for the innovativeness of rock to survive. It must always have an underground away from the mainstream. It must continue to push the boundaries of what is acceptable or unacceptable at any given moment in our society. And it must always contain some element that outrages and is outrageous. That is what makes it all such an amazing story—the story of rock 'n' roll.

A sock hop, fifties style.

IN
THE
BEGINNING

THE ROOTS OF ROCK 'N' ROLL

The roots of rock 'n' roll are deep and widespread. You can find them in the work songs of Southern blacks. You can find them in the twangy warbling of Texas swing or pure Nashville country. In big cities. In rural towns. In simple folk tunes. In sophisticated jazz. Rock 'n' roll prototypes are everywhere. They encompass the entire nation. Every geographic locale, every ethnic influence is represented. And that is why it is a unique American form—the Great Melting Pot.

Think of it: Immigrants from every corner of the globe taking a piece of their culture and native music with them on their journey to the New World. Passed along from generation to generation, these sounds intermingle, alter, grow, and diversify. Then two technological advances of the twentieth century accelerate the entire process. The radio and the phonograph record introduce countless listeners to various types and styles of music that they barely knew existed. In this atmosphere, the rock 'n' roll brew began bubbling, but there is more to it than that.

It was the early fifties, and America had rebounded from the hardships and sacrifices of World War II with a burst of affluence and technology unrivaled in this or any other century. One of the side effects of this thriving economy was the evolution of the American "teenager"—a creature unlike any previous inhabitant of the planet Earth. This variation of the species created a virtual subculture distinguishable from all the rest by its style of dress, manner of speech, choice of hairstyle, type of dance, and, most of all, its preferred music. That music was rock 'n' roll.

It is not surprising that this new breed of young person rejected outright the previously available pop music. The popularity charts were littered with sappy ballads, cute novelty songs, and lushly orchestrated music. Songs such as "Oh! My Pa-Pa," "How Much Is That Doggie in the Window," and "Three Coins in the Fountain" by artists such as Eddie Fisher, Patti Page, and the Four Aces. Nothing intrinsically wrong with any of them, but very little for fifties teenagers to sink their teeth into. And worse yet, very little to dance to.

It was the pursuit of energetic dance music that led young people to sample the exotic music being played on radio stations that were aimed primarily at black listeners. They voiced their pleasure with what they heard by going out in droves and buying records by the artists who made that music, which did not sit well with the adult community.

In the beginning, rock 'n' roll was perceived as a threat to the established order, and of course that is exactly what it was. Sometimes explicitly, sometimes implicitly, rock 'n' roll tested limits and challenged authority. It questioned previously unshakable attitudes and undermined fundamental assumptions about sex, religion, politics, even life itself. And if all that seems too grandiose to ascribe to a single three-chord form of popular music, remember, too, that above all else, and perhaps most diabolical of all, rock 'n' roll was fun—pure, simple, unadulterated fun. As America tumbled headlong into this uncharted era of peace and prosperity, rock 'n' roll music was the thread with which a whole generation would compile an identity for itself—one that continues to have appeal for succeeding generations to this very day.

Society at large certainly did not put out the welcome mat for rock 'n' roll. In fact, the Establishment mounted its best effort to thwart the onslaught of this new music. In addition to the expected tirades against rock by political, religious, and civic leaders, it is interesting to note that even those industries that had the most to gain from the future success and longevity of rock 'n' roll—radio, record companies, and broadcast trade magazines—were in dire, frantic opposition to it.

In New York, WCBS disc jockey Bob Haymes called rock 'n' roll ". . . poor music, badly recorded, with lyrics that are at best in bad taste, and at worst obscene. This trend in music (and I apologize for calling it music) is affecting the ideas and the lives of our children."

On the West Coast, a deejay in Los Angeles put it more succinctly when he said, "All rhythm and blues records are dirty, and as bad for kids as dope."

Even the music business trade paper *Cashbox* asked, "How long will it last? It is our guess that it won't."

So much for expert opinions. Closer to the truth was the 1958 observation by a South Philly combo called Danny and the Juniors that "Rock 'n' roll is here to stay. It will never die. It was meant to be that way. But I don't know why."

It would be a terrible conceit to think that any one person, place, or event was solely responsible for the rise of rock 'n' roll. It was more like a time-delayed chain reaction. Following is a handful of vitally significant components that had the cumulative effect of catapulting rock 'n' roll into the national consciousness.

THE MEDIA CONNECTION

"The Golden Age of Radio" describes the period of our history from about 1925 to 1945, when network radio enjoyed a kind of success undreamed of by its pioneers and unprecedented in the annals of world communication. The world had never seen or heard anything quite like it. Sounds of every variety appeared literally out of thin air, delivered right into our homes. There was a magic and excitement about it all. Comedy, variety, drama, music, news and quiz programs all found successful and sustaining berths in this new medium. Jack Benny, Fred Allen, Bing Crosby, Edgar Bergen and Charlie McCarthy, Bob Hope, and the Lone Ranger are just a few of the legendary names that kept America home and listening for more than twenty years, right through World War II. But then something new came along.

The arrival of television in the late forties and early fifties radically altered the nature of radio as it had been. Talent and advertisers on every rung of the broadcast ladder were lured away from radio by television's promise of greener pastures. Virtually overnight, big and small stations alike faced the very real possibility of extinction. Robbed of content, revenue, and national stature, radio was forced to localize and become a service medium. Music, talk, and news in varying combinations and formats established an enduring formula that survives intact today.

Individual stations began programming a particular kind of music twenty-four hours a day. There were classical stations and jazz stations and stations that played only those songs that appeared on the popularity charts. This came to be known as Top 40 radio, a format that was pioneered in 1949 by a man named Todd Storz in Omaha, Nebraska, but it soon spread like wildfire across the entire country. At the center of this type of programming was the disc jockey. And because of radio's immediacy and intimacy, the deejay became a force to be reckoned with in the entertainment industry—capable of making or breaking hit records and star performers, and of altering the direction of American popular music. One disc jockey in particular assumed this stature when he began to champion the rise of rock 'n' roll.

Alan Freed was an unlikely candidate to lead the rock revolution. While attending Ohio State University in the forties, he played trombone in a jazz band called the Sultans of Swing. After a stint in the military, he began his career as a disc jockey at a classical music station in New Castle, Pennsylvania. In 1946 he moved from there to Akron, Ohio, where his "Request Review" became a very popular program. He decided to move once again—this time to Cleveland—in 1950. It was there, at station

WJW, playing the pop hits of the day, that Freed became aware of the phenomenon of white teenagers dancing to rhythm and blues records and buying them in great numbers. Sensing the implications, he convinced his employers to allow him to play this music and promote it to a white audience. He called it rock 'n' roll (a term that had its origins in the lyrics of several R&B recordings as a euphemism for making love). It was an instant sensation.

Using Todd Rhodes's King recording "Blues for a Moon Dog" as a theme, Freed played records by the Orioles, the Moonglows, Billy Ward and the Dominoes featuring Clyde McPhatter, Tiny Grimes, and Jimmy "Night Train" Forest, among others. At first, Freed called himself Moondog—until legally stopped by a New York street musician who had used the name before him. With his gravelly voice and hip jargon, not to mention the music he played, Freed was presumed to be black by the majority of his vast listening audience. But his fame and popularity spread so quickly that it wasn't long before people in Cleveland and elsewhere knew Freed's real story. It was a story that would soon be repeated all across the country and around the world.

Alan Freed's success most certainly did not escape the attention of the major media centers. He moved to New York in 1954 and became a fixture at radio station WINS. A clue to his impact can be found in this excerpt from a September 24, 1972, *New York Times* article by Clark Whelton: "I was driving through Rocky Hill, twisting the dial on my car radio, when suddenly we picked up WINS and Freed, and zap!—we were hooked. In 1954 radio was Gruen watch commercials, soap operas, and Snooky Lanson 'Your Hit Parade' music. . . . Alan Freed jumped into radio like a stripper into *Swan Lake*. Someone later said that listening to Freed was like having an aisle seat for the San Francisco earthquake. Only it was better than that. Freed knocked down the buildings you hated and turned the rest into dance floors. In 1954 there was no one like him."

Hollywood also beckoned, and between 1956 and 1959, Freed

Alan Freed, the first
rock 'n' roll disc jockey

made a series of motion pictures, basically playing himself as the defender of rock 'n' roll to any and all who would listen—in between performances by Bill Haley, Chuck Berry, Little Richard, Frankie Lymon, and the like. In addition, there were television programs—network and local—as well as a series of legendary live stage shows that paved the way for the modern-day rock concert as we know it. It seemed for a while as if Alan Freed could do no wrong.

One of Freed's associates at WINS, Paul Sherman, recalled their first encounter. "I see this guy sitting in the studio with a big telephone book in front of an open microphone, thumping his hand all the while the record was playing and making gibbering noises in the background: 'Go, man, go,' and 'Yeah, yeah, yeah,' and other sounds I can't reproduce. He was accompanying the music, accenting the beat. Lew Fisher and I were working on the night shift and we were next door. We looked at each other, and Fisher said, 'Oh my God, I give him three months.' I said, 'You're crazy. I give him one week.' "

They couldn't have been more wrong.

THE BREAKTHROUGH

We've already mentioned probably the most famous recording session of all time for "We Are the World" in 1985. There was another rather remarkable session that took place more than three decades earlier on April 12, 1954, in a small studio in New York City. Only for this one, there were no film crews on hand to greet the participants, no photographers recording every move for posterity. Luckily, tape recorders were turning to capture the sounds being made that night, but even these seemed destined for anonymity when the record resulting from that session was released and went nowhere. It was called "Rock Around the Clock" by Bill Haley and the Comets.

Bill Haley was born on July 6, 1925, in Highland Park, Michigan. He made his first record at the age of eighteen and went out on the road as a singer and guitarist with several different country and western bands. One of his groups, the Saddlemen, recorded a cover version of Jackie Brenston's 1951 R&B hit,

"Rocket 88." The record did not sell well, but it did convince Haley that black music was the way to go. In 1952 he changed the name of his group to Bill Haley and the Comets and had moderate success with songs such as "Rock the Joint" and "Crazy Man Crazy" on Essex Records. In 1954 the group switched to the Decca label and recorded "Rock Around the Clock."

It wasn't until a full year later, when filmmaker Richard Brooks chose the song to underscore the theme of youthful rebellion in his motion picture *The Blackboard Jungle*, that the song heralded rock 'n' roll's first major impact on American popular

Bill Haley (third from right) and the Comets.

culture. Like so many fads before or since, it could have been just a fluke, an aberration, a one-time-only assault on the staid traditions of Tin Pan Alley—but it wasn't. "Rock Around the Clock" planted rock 'n' roll's flag on the Top 40 charts and staked a claim that has lasted very nearly unchallenged for more than thirty years and shows no signs of stopping or even slowing down.

THE SEX SYMBOL

On January 28, 1956, exactly twenty-nine years before the U.S.A. for Africa recording, I was at home with my father when he called me frantically from the living room to come join him. All I knew was that he was watching a television program hosted by Tommy and Jimmy Dorsey called "Stage Show." As a product of the Big Band era, he was the proud owner of an extensive collection of 78-r.p.m. records by all of the greats—Benny Goodman, Artie Shaw, Glenn Miller, and, of course, the Dorsey Brothers. But on this particular evening, he was not calling me to listen to Big Band music. In fact, without even knowing it, he was calling me to witness the birth of a brand-new era in musical history. It was the national television debut of a former truck driver from Memphis, Tennessee, by the name of Elvis Presley.

I remember liking Elvis right away. There was something about the way he looked, something about the way he sang, something about the way he moved that was unlike anything I had ever seen before on television or anywhere else. And I wanted to see and hear more.

How can one even begin to hint at the importance of Elvis to rock 'n' roll? Elvis Presley was clearly one of the most pivotal figures in the history of American music and popular culture. Yet, there is nothing in his unremarkable early years that prefigured the impact he would have later on in life. He was born on January 8, 1935, in East Tupelo, Mississippi. His twin brother was stillborn, so Elvis grew up an only child, devoted to his parents, Vernon and Gladys Presley. In 1948 the family moved to Memphis and Elvis became exposed to local black bluesmen such as Furry Lewis and B. B. King. After graduating from high school in 1953, Elvis worked for a tool company and then drove a truck for a local electric company. Sometime that summer, according to the legend, Elvis showed up at the doorstep of Sun Records in Memphis, where anyone could make a demonstration recording of themselves for four dollars.

"If I could find a white man who had the Negro sound and the Negro feel, I could make a billion dollars," Sam Phillips, the owner of Sun Records, was quoted as saying in the early fifties. Elvis Presley was the fulfillment of Sam Phillips's wish—and then some. His emergence in the mid-fifties struck like lightning. He raised eyebrows, he raised temperatures, and he raised awareness of rock 'n' roll to greater and greater heights. Part of it was the way he looked: the long sideburns, the ducktail haircut, the piercing bedroom eyes, and the perpetual sneer. Part of it was the way he moved onstage: totally uninhibited, body quivering, hips swiveling to the steady beat of the music. Elvis's appearances on network television sent shockwaves throughout the entire country. In one memorable outing on "The Ed Sullivan Show" in 1957, Elvis was only allowed to be seen from the waist up!

Admittedly, there is a case to be made that Elvis Presley's rock 'n' roll dynamism came to an abrupt end with his induction into

The King of
Rock 'n' Roll.

the Army in 1958, and the subsequent death of his mother while he was overseas in Germany. Also, the turbulent sixties took rock 'n' roll in directions that even Elvis couldn't begin to relate to, let alone participate in. But all of this pales in the face of the indelible mark that Elvis left on the hearts and minds of millions of fans *and* the thousands of musicians who followed in his wake.

As a result, nothing can take away or diminish Elvis Presley's place in rock 'n' roll history. Not the shocking deterioration of his physical appearance or the tragic circumstances surrounding his death. Not the unmerciful posthumous merchandising and repackaging of his legend. Not the long string of regrettable, forgettable motion pictures. Not even the way he rested on his laurels through much of his career. The simple truth is that in the beginning Elvis Presley *was* rock 'n' roll, in the same way that Babe Ruth was baseball and Charles Lindbergh was aviation. Not in any self-conscious, analytical, intellectual way, but rather on the level of pure instinct and accomplishment. His arrival on the scene gave this burgeoning music a mesmerizing, charismatic focal point—a hook on which to hang the dreams and fantasies of the youth of the nation.

Elvis may be dead and gone, but the dreams and fantasies live on. Those who experienced the phenomenon firsthand will always hold a special place in their hearts for the Elvis of their youth and adolescence. But what if you're interested in examining the precursor of your own heroes? Fortunately, in a media age, this would not be too difficult to accomplish. In fact, an anthology of his greatest hits ("Hound Dog," "Don't Be Cruel," "Jailhouse Rock," "Love Me Tender," et al), kinescopes of some early TV shows, one or two carefully chosen movies, and a copy

Elvis at the taping of his 1968 television special.

of his 1968 NBC television special should just about do it.

With the wisdom of hindsight, nothing showcased Elvis better than that 1968 special. It came at the perfect time for him. Following his discharge from the Army in 1960, he spent the next eight years almost totally isolated from his adoring public, releasing albums and singles on a carefully prescribed schedule and making two or three of those lighter-than-air movies a year. By 1968 he was restless and bored. In January of that year, it was announced that Elvis had signed to do a Christmastime television special for NBC. It was the intention of his domineering manager, Colonel Tom Parker, that Elvis perform an hour of holiday songs. But producer-director Steve Binder had other ideas. He envisioned Elvis's name in lights twenty feet high, powerful production numbers, and a musical retrospective tracing Elvis's career all the way from the beginning. Fortunately, Binder's vision prevailed.

The taping took place in June. Binder's approach afforded Elvis a way back to live performing and contact with an audience. He more than met the challenge. The centerpiece of the special was an in-the-round concert performance by Elvis before a live audience. Dressed head-to-toe in black leather, he looked terrific—at the peak of his handsomeness and physical development, his smoldering sensuality and mesmerizing effect on an audience intact. The even better news was that he sounded as good as he looked. Shy, but totally self-confident. Reticent, but nonetheless speaking volumes with a glance or a gesture.

He reminisced with his original backup musicians, joked with members of the audience, and delivered a steady stream of the rock 'n' roll gospel according to Elvis. Watching the tape all these many years later, it is quite apparent that he knew he still had it. And what's more, he knew that we knew that he knew he still had it. The program climaxed with Elvis, in a white suit this time, standing in front of those twenty-foot-high letters, belting out an anthem about brotherhood commissioned especially for the program entitled "If I Can Dream."

The special aired on Tuesday, December 3, 1968. By the time it was over, Elvis had clearly reclaimed his title as the King of Rock 'n' Roll—a title he would take with him to eternity less than ten years later on August 16, 1977.

THE INNOVATORS

Chuck Berry

Elvis was a figurehead—the front man for this new mode of music and behavior. Right behind him were the innovators: the architects, designers, and sculptors of the art of rock 'n' roll. First and foremost among them was Chuck Berry.

There is nothing more recognizable as the pure essence of rock 'n' roll than a Chuck Berry guitar riff. Whether it's played by the master himself, or in a loving tribute by the Rolling Stones, or even by some amateur bar band on a Saturday night, the look, sound, and sensibility of a Chuck Berry song tell just about all there is to know about the content and concerns of rock 'n' roll.

Charles Edward Berry was born in St. Louis, Missouri, on October 18, 1926. He learned to play the guitar as a teenager, and by 1955 he was one of the most popular St. Louis area musicians. In May of that year he met the legendary bluesman Muddy Waters, who introduced him to Leonard Chess of Chess Records.

Chuck Berry doing his famous "duckwalk."

In a 1979 radio interview, Berry recalled this meeting: "He [Leonard Chess] said, 'Why don't you bring your group up and record and I'll give you a contract.' So, on May 21, 1955, with Ebby Harding, Johnnie Johnson, and myself—that's drums, piano, and guitar—and he added Willie Dixon on bass, we recorded 'Maybellene,' 'Wee Wee Hours,' 'Too Much Monkey Business,' and 'Roll Over Beethoven.' And from there it's pretty much in the history book."

From someone else, that statement might seem like a gross exaggeration. From Chuck Berry, it's the absolute truth. His songs were anthems for the new music and new consciousness that was beginning to permeate the land. Witness this lyric from "School Day (Ring! Ring! Goes the Bell)":

Hail, hail rock 'n' roll.
Deliver me from the days of old.
Long live rock 'n' roll.
The beat of the drums loud and bold.
Rock, rock, rock 'n' roll.
The feeling is there, body and soul.

In all of his best songs, Chuck Berry had the uncanny knack of placing his finger squarely on the pulse of the American teenager—crossing all kinds of ethnic, social, and economic boundaries in the process. Framed by the clanging guitar style that inspired an army of musicians and made all the more irresistible by a charming sense of humor and delightful stage presence—complete with his trademark "duckwalk"—Chuck Berry created a body of work that is as essential to a complete understanding of rock 'n' roll as anything by his peers or successors. That is why his catalog of songs remains one of the most active in all of popular music, with cover versions and hit remakes by just about every major star with rock 'n' roll aspirations in the last three decades, including the Beatles ("Roll Over Beethoven"), the Rolling Stones ("Carol"), the Beach Boys ("Rock and Roll Music"), the Grateful Dead ("Johnny B. Goode"), and Linda Ronstadt ("Back in the U.S.A.").

The Everly Brothers

An equally lasting contribution was made by two brothers from

Don and Phil Everly.

Kentucky. Steeped in the musical traditions of the Appalachian Mountains, Don and Phil Everly brought two-part country and western harmonies to rock 'n' roll. Their vocal style proved conclusively that rock wasn't just for gritty, rough-hewn vocalizing. That it could, in fact, be sensitive, sonorous, even downright pretty.

Don Everly was born on February 1, 1937, in Brownie, Kentucky. Phil Everly arrived on January 19, 1939. Through the years, the word most often used in describing the Everly Brothers is professionalism. This is not surprising. After all, they began their performing careers as youngsters with their midwestern country star parents, Ike and Margaret Everly. From that experience on, they surrounded themselves with other capable, seasoned professionals—in the recording studio and on the concert stage.

The Everly Brothers sang like choirboys. Their songs about love and teenage social life (including "Bye Bye Love," "Wake Up, Little Susie," "All I Have to Do Is Dream," and "Cathy's Clown") contained original instrumentation, adventurous production, and lyrics that struck a responsive chord in the minds and hearts of listeners around the globe. Just look at a partial list of artists who fervently acknowledge the Everlys as an influence and an inspiration: the Beatles, Simon and Garfunkel, the Buffalo Springfield, the Byrds, and, more recently, Dave Edmunds and Nick Lowe.

Unfortunately, the harmony in their music hasn't always been as evident in their personal lives. Their partnership came to a screeching halt onstage one night in Hollywood on July 14, 1973. For ten years, the brothers hardly even spoke to one another, let

One of the most flamboyant and controversial early rockers— Jerry Lee Lewis.

alone performed together. But then in September 1983 an emotional reunion took place onstage at the Albert Hall in London. Since that night, the Everly Brothers have once again been dispensing their own unique blend of rock 'n' roll medicine to their fans all over the world.

Writer Andy Wickham once recalled the extraordinary effect first hearing the Everly Brothers had on him: "I remember jumping up and down. I remember laughing a lot. I remember rushing madly to the radio and turning up the volume as far as it would go. I remember flinging all the windows open so that the neighbors, the cows in the field, and the eighty-year-old gardener trimming the shrubs out back could share this Elysian experience."

That feeling is forever-ly.

Buddy Holly

Buddy Holly was as unlikely a candidate for musical superstardom as there ever was. The "teen idols" to be might have all come from central casting with their dreamy eyes, good looks, and often amazing pompadours. But not so Buddy Holly. This tall and thin Texan with large black horn-rimmed glasses might never be mistaken for a movie star, but he paved the way for a number of innovations in rock 'n' roll that stand pretty much untampered with to this very day. First of all, he wrote or co-wrote most of his biggest hits. Second, he established the pattern for the basic self-contained rock 'n' roll combo: lead guitar, rhythm guitar, bass, and drums. Third, his vocal stylings and wide-ranging instrumentation gave his records their completely unique stamp of originality. And last, he was the first in the recording studio to make extensive use of overdubs and multi-tracking in rock 'n' roll (a process pioneered by the legendary guitarist Les Paul). Quite a number of impressive accomplishments for one who lived so short a life.

Charles Harden Holley was born on September 7, 1936, in Lubbock, Texas. Buddy was the youngest of four children in a very

Buddy Holly (center) and the Crickets.

musical family. He learned to play guitar from his older brothers, and by junior high school, he and his friends were playing "western and bop," as they called it, at local clubs and dances. But late at night, he kept his ear glued to the radio, listening to stations throughout the Southwest playing rhythm and blues music and early rock 'n' roll. Needless to say, he was impressed. When

Elvis Presley passed through Lubbock in 1955, Buddy's eyes and ears were opened to new possibilities and he began experimenting with various combinations of blues and country.

In 1956 Buddy traveled to Nashville to make his first recordings for Decca Records, which were unsuccessful largely because the label was pushing him in a pure country direction. Back in Lubbock, Buddy heard about a producer named Norman Petty who had his own studio in Clovis, New Mexico. In an atmosphere of total creative freedom, Buddy and his group, the Crickets, began recording the remarkable string of hits that brought them consistently to the top of the charts between 1957 and 1959. Like Chuck Berry's songs, the Buddy Holly catalog is *very* active. Coincidentally, all of the artists we mentioned earlier as recording Chuck Berry tunes have likewise recorded material by Buddy Holly: the Beatles ("Words of Love"), the Rolling Stones ("Not Fade Away"), the Beach Boys ("Peggy Sue"), the Grateful Dead ("Not Fade Away"), and Linda Ronstadt ("That'll Be the Day").

Even today those original recordings have lost none of their dynamism and power. The individual components may have been borrowed from many sources, but the overall sound and style was totally original—pure Buddy Holly and pure rock 'n' roll. There's no telling how far Buddy's curiosity and determination may have taken him. We'll never know. On February 3, 1959, Buddy Holly was killed in the crash of a private plane while on a tour of one-nighters in the Midwest. He was twenty-two years old.

Ironically, in death Holly remains eternally youthful—forever unaffected by changes in styles, sounds, technology, and trends. Unlike many of his contemporaries, he can never be victimized by the ravages of time or by the ebbs and flows of fortune. His legacy is set firmly in place. Over a quarter of a century after his death, Buddy Holly continues to be celebrated in books, movies, records, and videos for his all too brief but nevertheless lasting grasp on the heart of rock 'n' roll.

Dion

Another unlikely contender for rock 'n' roll greatness came from the streets of one of the five boroughs of the city of New York. You didn't have to be from the Bronx to appreciate Dion and the Belmonts—but it sure didn't hurt any!

After their first hit, "I Wonder Why," in 1958, my friends and I from nearby neighborhoods used to make pilgrimages over to Belmont Avenue, as if that street sign itself contained some magic or held the secret to our own destiny. It's no wonder we felt a special closeness to Dion. Elvis was totally out of reach. So were the Everly Brothers and Buddy Holly. But Dion was different. He was homegrown. There was always somebody around who shot pool with his cousin or went to school with his sister.

What was it about Dion—alone or with the Belmonts—that was so special? First of all, it is my contention that Dion DiMucci is one of the best male vocalists that rock 'n' roll has ever produced. Just listen to "Runaround Sue" or "The Wanderer." Second, there was his special brand of street singing, buffeted by those intriguing harmonies perfected with the Belmonts by utilizing the natural echo of a multitude of New York subway stations. In addition, Dion and the Belmonts bridged the gap between the music of their parents and the music of their peers like few other vocal groups could or did. Even a mother could love their versions of standard pop fare, such as "Where or When" or "When You Wish Upon a Star," which were originally written for a Broadway show and a Disney movie, respectively.

But more than all of that, Dion was an inspiration. He was living proof that with the right combination of street smarts and rock 'n' roll you could break away from the old neighborhood and do something with your life. And that inspiration wasn't just limited to the Bronx, either. Bruce Springsteen felt it over in New Jersey. And Brian Wilson felt it out in California. Even the Beatles felt it over in Liverpool: Haven't you noticed Dion's smiling face on the cover of *Sgt. Pepper's Lonely Hearts Club Band?*

Little Richard

Another seminal figure in the birth of rock 'n' roll was a young man from Macon, Georgia, named Richard Penniman. Little Richard, as he came to be known in the fifties, heard the sounds of a different drummer in his head. He sang those sounds in a controversial, revolutionary way. In that regard, he established the formula for legions of rock 'n' roll songwriters and performers who came after him. He understood intuitively that part of rock's appeal had nothing to do with traditional song lyrics and sentiments. The energy and vitality of the performance were far more important than the words. Songs such as "Tutti Fruiti" and "Long Tall Sally" settled snugly in the emotions of the listener.

With his maniacal, screaming vocals and urgent sensuality, Richard was thought to be too aggressively sexual and threaten-

The "sedate" piano style of Little Richard.

ing for the white sensibility. And so, his material was originally exposed to the mass audience in laundered versions by mainstream artists such as Pat Boone. This was the case with his "Tutti Fruiti" and also with Fats Domino's "Blueberry Hill." It was not uncommon at the time. Until the rock dam burst wide open, tame cover versions of rip-roaring rock classics were a fact of life. White vocal groups often remade black doo-wop records, and because they had easier access to radio airplay, the cover versions often outsold the originals. "Sh-Boom (Life Could Be a Dream)" by the white Crew Cuts did much better than "Sh-Boom (Life Could Be a Dream)" by the black Chords. "Work with Me, Annie" by Hank Ballard and the Midnighters (a song clearly about sex) was altered to "Dance with Me, Henry" by Georgia Gibbs and became a big hit. And so on.

Another negative lesson learned from the career of Little Richard is one equally applicable to a variety of other artists who all had a few things in common. Many were young, black, inexperienced in business matters, and poorly educated. As such, they were easy targets for unfair contracts, creative accounting, and purloined publishing. As a result, they were cheated out of millions of dollars in royalties and other earnings. Since many of them did not maintain the kind of careers and visibility that might overcome such a handicap, they suffered tremendous economic consequences from which they could never fully recover.

No one was immune from these abuses. To this day, if you look at the songwriter credit for Chuck Berry's "Maybellene," you will see the name Alan Freed listed as a co-author. This is certainly not to suggest that Chuck Berry needed any help in writing his rock 'n' roll classics. But he did need help to get them on the radio. And it was business as usual at the time for an entrepreneur of Freed's stature to receive songwriting credit—and the resulting financial rewards—in return for the precious airplay they could provide. Only recently did Little Richard sue his early business associates for unpaid royalties and other contractual irregularities. At this writing, the case is still pending. Surely there were white artists who were taken advantage of as well. But this scourge of racism that dangles over rock 'n' roll is a blot on its generally progressive record in the handling of racial matters.

YEARS
OF
TRANSITION

The conventional wisdom is that rock 'n' roll fell on hard times in the late fifties and early sixties. The usual litany of evidence offered to support this theory goes as follows:

- Elvis was in the Army and the Everly Brothers were in the Marines.
- Little Richard abandoned rock 'n' roll for the ministry.
- Chuck Berry spent some time in prison on a morals charge.
- Jerry Lee Lewis incurred the wrath of just about everybody for marrying his thirteen-year-old second cousin.
- Buddy Holly was dead.

Then, too, there was payola.

Payola was the word coined to describe the act of paying (or otherwise financially rewarding) a disc jockey to play a particular record. We have already seen an example of the practice in the co-author credit given to Alan Freed for a Chuck Berry song. A more blatant example of payola involved the actual exchange of cash for airplay—most often from the large or small record company itself directly to the disc jockey or other person who chose what got played on the air.

So payola did affect—and restrict—airplay, and thus influenced both record sales and the public's taste. In addition, exposing and punishing payola gave many powerful elements of the Establishment—old-line music publishers, congressional committees, etc.—the opportunity to attack rock 'n' roll for the sham they thought it was.

In 1959 a House Legislative Oversight Committee broadened its investigation of corrupt broadcasting practices, which had centered on rigged television game shows, to include payola. Then, on May 19, 1960, a grand jury in New York indicted eight broadcasters for what amounted to taking bribes. The biggest name among them was Alan Freed.

Freed denied the charges. "I've never taken a bribe," he said. "If I've helped somebody, I'll accept a nice gift, but I wouldn't take a dime to plug a record. . . . Somebody said to me once, 'If somebody sent you a Cadillac, would you send it back?' I said, 'It depends on the color.'" Responses like that didn't help his cause much. Freed lost both his radio and television shows in New York and spent the rest of his life trying to repair the damage done to his career, his finances, and his reputation. He never made it. Alan Freed died of a liver disorder associated with heavy drinking on January 20, 1965.

The payola scandal had a chilling effect on the radio industry.

Most stations reacted by tightening their formats and centralizing control over what got played on the air in the hands of a program or music director. The end result was an overall sanitizing of the music we call rock 'n' roll. Fewer chances were taken on new artists and unknown commodities for fear of their motivation being called into question.

All things considered, it definitely was a dark time for rock 'n' roll, but it was by no means terminal or even life-threatening. Any look at the charts for the years 1959–63 will show that great rock 'n' roll records continued to appear on a steady basis—even if the process did become more formularized. Nonetheless, there were good things going on all over the place.

First of all, starting with "Sherry" in 1962, a group from New Jersey called the Four Seasons began placing their phenomenal string of Top 40 singles on the U.S. charts. Also, fabulous husband-and-wife songwriting teams were cranking out nonstop hits:

- Gerry Goffin and Carole King wrote classics such as "Will You Love Me Tomorrow?," "Up on the Roof," and "The Loco-Motion."
- Barry Mann and Cynthia Weil wrote "On Broadway," "We Gotta Get Out of This Place," and "You've Lost That Lovin' Feelin'. "
- And Ellie Greenwich and Jeff Barry were responsible for "Be My Baby," "Da Doo Ron Ron (When He Walked Me Home)," and "Hanky Panky."

Meanwhile, the so-called "girl groups" were proving conclusively that rock 'n' roll was not exclusively a man's world. White

The Supremes—
Mary Wilson,
Diana Ross,
Florence Ballard—
at the peak
of their hit-making
success.

or black, large or small, these women left an indelible mark on rock 'n' roll. They were the female equivalent of all the great street corner doo-wop singing groups of the fifties. On record and onstage, they celebrated the basics of teenage existence—youth, good times, sexual awakening, heartbreak, and, most of all, boyfriends! A dozen of the best include:

- the Angels: "My Boyfriend's Back"
- the Chantels: "Maybe"
- the Chiffons: "He's So Fine"
- the Crystals: "Da Doo Ron Ron (When He Walked Me Home)"
- the Dixie Cups: "Chapel of Love"
- the Essex: "Easier Said Than Done"
- Martha and the Vandellas: "Dancing in the Street"
- the Marvelettes: "Please Mister Postman"
- the Ronettes: "Be My Baby"
- the Shangri-Las: "Leader of the Pack"
- the Shirelles: "Will You Love Me Tomorrow?"
- the Supremes: Just about anything by them.

Dance crazes—spearheaded by the Twist, but also including the Boogaloo, the Frug, the Funky Chicken, the Jerk, the Mashed Potato, the Monkey, the Pony, the Swim, and the Watusi—swept the country in the early sixties. And teen idols (it seems like most of them were named Bobby) kept putting hits on the charts and palpitations in the hearts of their female fans. In addition to activity on all of these fronts, the seeds were planted and nurtured for three phenomena that had an impressive impact on the rock 'n' roll of their day, and, what is more astonishing, a continuing influence on the rock 'n' roll of today: Phil Spector, Motown, and the Beach Boys.

PHIL SPECTOR

What impresses one first even after all these years is the sheer size of the sound. Phil Spector applied the cinematic techniques of an epic moviemaker, such as Cecil B. De Mille, to rock 'n' roll. It was pure spectacle. To say that the production on early rock 'n' roll records was sparse is an understatement. Phil Spector productions, on the other hand, were full of bombast and fury. It was called "The Wall of Sound." Overdubs were piled on top of overdubs until the end result nearly registered on a seismograph.

Phil Spector was born on the day after Christmas, 1940, in the Bronx, New York. He moved to Los Angeles at the age of twelve. In 1958 Spector and two friends formed a trio called the Teddy Bears. Their first hit—and Spector's first production—was a song called "To Know Him Is to Love Him" a title taken from the inscription on his father's gravestone.

In 1960 Spector returned to New York to work for songwriters Jerry Lieber and Mike Stoller, with whom he co-wrote the Top 10 single "Spanish Harlem" for Ben E. King. By early 1962 he had formed his own label—Philles Records—and began churning out hit after hit after hit, including the Crystals' "He's a Rebel," "Da Doo Ron Ron (When He Walked Me Home)," and "Then He Kissed Me"; the Ronettes' "Be My Baby," "Baby, I Love You," and "Walking in the Rain"; Darlene Love's " (Today I Met) The Boy I'm Gonna Marry" and "Wait Till My Bobby Gets Home"; and the Righteous Brothers' "You've Lost That Lovin' Feelin'."

Spector's work as a producer alone would have assured his

Phil Spector—
the Tycoon of Teen.

place in rock 'n' roll history. But his preeminence did not end with the sound of his records. There was no aspect of the entire process of making and marketing a record that he was not involved in—from talent acquisition to publicity and promotion. In that quest for total control, Spector undermined the established methods of doing business in the recording industry. For this, he was dubbed the Tycoon of Teen—and with good reason. A millionaire at twenty-one, Spector established the pattern for every young rock entrepreneur since.

Unfortunately, his talents were more than matched by his eccentricities. Even at the height of his success, he lived as a virtual recluse in his twenty-three room Hollywood mansion. One incident in particular led to his withdrawal from the record business. In 1966, following the failure of one of his most exciting productions, "River Deep—Mountain High" by Ike and Tina Turner, he went into semiretirement. There's been an occasional project since, including a controversial involvement with the Beatles, but Spector's greater glory these days can be found in the hands of his heirs and successors. "The Wall of Sound" is alive and well in the work of Bruce Springsteen, Billy Joel, Meat Loaf, Daryl Hall and John Oates.

MOTOWN

If Phil Spector has a black counterpart in sixties rock, it would have to be Berry Gordy. Like Spector, Gordy could write songs, produce records, scout talent, and promote hits, but ultimately it was his business acumen that was most responsible for building the empire we know today as Motown. Starting out in Detroit in the mid-fifties, Gordy began developing a synthesis of black and white music that would reach its peak a decade later. It started modestly enough. With the profits accumulated from writing a few hits and leasing a few master recordings to the major labels, Gordy pooled his resources and started a label of his own. With an almost unerring eye and ear for talent, Gordy's first signing was a local Detroit quintet called the Miracles, whose lead singer and songwriter, Smokey Robinson, can be counted among the finest musical craftsmen in all of popular music.

After a couple of modest successes, the Miracles hit paydirt with a song called "Shop Around" that reached number two on the national singles charts in 1961. The floodgates were opened. This first major hit gave Gordy the resources to pursue his unique musical vision. His goal was to create a team of writers, producers, and artists who could apply the same techniques to music that Gordy had observed on the auto assembly lines of Detroit. The strategy worked beautifully. As distinctive as each artist was, there was a consistency and familiarity to each and every record they made. This was partly due to the fact that each group drew from the same pool of highly talented Detroit studio musicians. This was the legendary Motown Sound—something very special and unique—a combination of pop and soul that captivated listeners around the globe and still does, well over two decades later. That power has not diminished with the passing of time. Evidence of its influence is everywhere: Mick Jagger and David Bowie doing a rousing cover version of "Dancing in the Street" or Eddie Kendricks and David Ruffin bringing the house down at Live Aid when they joined Hall and Oates onstage for a Motown medley. Motown's impact is felt even in the most widespread of the mass media. When NBC telecast the compa-

Motown mogul
Berry Gordy.

ny's "25th Anniversary Special" in 1983, it was number one in
the ratings that week. All in all, a great tribute to a remarkable
family of artists. Among the best were:

The Four Tops originally got together sometime around 1953
in Detroit. After joining Motown in 1964, they were united with
the in-house writing and producing team of Brian Holland,

Lamont Dozier, and Eddie Holland, resulting in a laundry list of Top 40 hits, including "Baby, I Need Your Loving," "I Can't Help Myself (Sugar Pie, Honey Bunch)," "It's the Same Old Song," and "Reach Out I'll Be There."

The Temptations: David Ruffin, Melvin Franklin, Paul Williams, Otis Williams, Eddie Kendricks.

Marvin Gaye was heard by Berry Gordy while playing a club date in Detroit in 1961. His early Top 10 hits included "Pride and Joy," "I'll Be Doggone," "Ain't That Peculiar," and "How Sweet It Is to Be Loved by You."

Martha Reeves was a secretary in the A&R (artists and repertoire) department at Motown. She began singing backup vocals on Motown sessions and ultimately fronted her own group, Martha and the Vandellas. Their Holland–Dozier–Holland-composed hits included "Heat Wave," "Dancing in the Street," and "Nowhere to Run."

The original Supremes—Diana Ross, Florence Ballard, and Mary Wilson—racked up an unheard of dozen number one singles on the U.S. charts: "Where Did Our Love Go?"; "Baby Love"; "Come See About Me"; "Stop! In the Name of Love"; "Back in My Arms Again"; "I Hear a Symphony"; "You Can't Hurry Love"; "You Keep Me Hangin' On"; "Love Is Here and Now You're Gone"; "The Happening"; "Love Child"; and "Someday We'll Be Together." Quite simply, the Supremes were the most successful female group of the sixties.

The Temptations were easily one of the most successful male groups of the sixties, a male equivalent of the Supremes at Motown. The group evolved over a period of years, but it wasn't until they started working with writer-producer Smokey Robinson that the Tempts began their unbroken string of hit records with songs such as "The Way You Do the Things You Do" and "My Girl" and later on with the Norman Whitfield–Brian Holland productions "Ain't Too Proud to Beg," "Beauty Is Only Skin Deep," and "(I Know) I'm Losing You."

Steveland Morris, blind from birth, was born on May 13, 1950, in Saginaw, Michigan. Ronnie White of the Miracles discovered him and introduced him to Berry Gordy, who changed his name to Little Stevie Wonder in recognition of his musical genius. His third Motown single, "Fingertips (Part II)," went to number one in 1963. From that point on, Stevie Wonder has grown up before our eyes and ears, surpassing every expectation that any reasonable person could have imagined for him.

No doubt about it, one expects such talented performers to produce prodigiously. But Motown's accomplishment goes beyond that. An astounding 75 percent of the singles released by Motown landed on the national pop charts. That hit ratio by a recording company is unequaled.

And Gordy's personal achievement is even more impressive. After years of fears in the record industry about white audiences accepting black music, Gordy was responsible for the widest and warmest reception of black music by audiences of any· racial makeup anywhere in the world. And with the major creative and technical roles at Motown being handled by blacks, a dramatic statement in its own right was being declared loudly and proudly in the civil-rights-conscious sixties.

THE BEACH BOYS

One of the most incredible and longest-lasting success stories in American rock 'n' roll (or any other form of popular music, for that matter) is the saga of three brothers, their cousin, and a family friend from Hawthorne, California, who called themselves the Beach Boys. It is a multifaceted story filled with dreams and triumph on one side, nightmares and tragedy on the other. It began simply enough with the songs of surfing, cars, girls, and school spirit fashioned together largely through the talents and vision of the eldest of the three brothers—Brian Wilson. What set Brian's efforts apart from his peers' was his uncanny ability to express the longings, fantasies, and deep emotions of teenagers in his songs. It was this content, coupled with

The Beach Boys
(clockwise
from top):
Brian Wilson,
Carl Wilson,
Mike Love,
Al Jardine,
Dennis Wilson.

the sweetest five-part male harmony ever attempted in a rock 'n' roll framework, that secured Brian his place in music history.

For the record, Brian, Carl, and Dennis Wilson were all born in Hawthorne in 1942, 1944, and 1946, respectively. Mike Love was born in Los Angeles in 1941 and Al Jardine in Lima, Ohio, in 1942. On the suggestion of Dennis Wilson in 1961, Brian Wilson and Mike Love wrote a song called "Surfin'" that became a regional hit on the small independent Candix label. In 1962 the group switched to Capitol Records and began their run of hit records that kept them steadily on the charts for the next half decade, including "Surfin' U.S.A.," "I Get Around," and "Good Vibrations." Joyous rock 'n' roll, coupled with bittersweet ballads, was the formula the Beach Boys employed on their albums, which were produced from very early on by Brian Wilson. Both in business and personal terms, it was very rare at the time for one single young musician to take such total control of a group. But, as the late Dennis Wilson said in 1977, "Brian Wilson *is* the Beach Boys. He is the band. We are his messengers."

Caught in the creativity explosion of the sixties, Brian pushed harder and harder to achieve greater success. In the aftermath of Beatlemania, the pressures caught up with him and he suffered a nervous breakdown around Christmastime in 1964. As a result, he stopped touring with the group and concentrated on plotting the Beach Boys' musical future. The result of these efforts in May 1966 was the release of one of the greatest albums in rock 'n' roll history, *Pet Sounds*. In this major undertaking, Brian subtly but masterfully explored the thin line between adolescence and adulthood with compassion and total empathy.

Even Paul McCartney acknowledged this in a 1980 interview

with *Musician* magazine: "A big influence was *Pet Sounds* by the Beach Boys. That was the album that flipped me. Still does, actually. Still one of my favorite albums of all time. Just because the musical invention on that is like, 'Wow!' But that was the big thing for me. I just thought, 'Oh, dear me, the album of all time. What the hell are we going to do?'"

By the late sixties, however, the Beach Boys had fallen on hard times. Seemingly out of step with the hippie psychedelic music in fashion at the time, the group was ridiculed and basically dismissed in America during those years. They concentrated instead on performing in Europe, where their popularity never waned. Slowly but surely in the early seventies, the group began its creative and commercial renaissance. Then the unexpected occurred. In 1974, with Vietnam and Watergate behind us, America was ready to have fun again. A new generation of young people embraced the Beach Boy philosophy of sun, fun, and freedom. An anthology of their best early work, *Endless Summer*, became the number one album in the U.S. in October 1974. Since then the Beach Boys have remained a consistently popular touring attraction, while sporadically releasing moderately successful albums of new material. And therein lies the dilemma.

Through a combination of Brian's mental and emotional problems, continual in-group fighting and personality clashes, the death by drowning of Dennis Wilson while legally intoxicated in 1983, and a revolving door of managers, record companies, and business entanglements throughout their career, the Beach Boys remain much more important for what they once were rather than for what they are or could be. Still, there must always be, for the group and their truest fans, consolation in the realization that, no matter what happens from here on out,

Brian Wilson, in the relatively brief period from 1961 to 1967, created a body of work that has withstood the test of time and continues to be irresistible to succeeding generations of young people.

With all this activity beginning to germinate in the music of the early sixties, things were never quite as drastic as they are often portrayed in the rock histories. There were performers and fans alike keeping the faith, but no doubt some of the early glow and excitement was gone. The prevailing attitude seemed to be: If you can't lick 'em, join 'em. And so a good deal of rock 'n' roll's outrageousness and rebellion was diffused by its inclusion in the Establishment's method of doing things. On the whole, rock became less exciting in direct proportion to its becoming more acceptable. As one of the main characters says in the film *American Graffiti*, set in 1962, "Rock 'n' roll's been going downhill ever since Buddy Holly died."

In addition, you cannot separate the content of a nation's popular music from the reality of what is going on in the society. The kinds of social upheaval that would dominate the middle and late sixties were still in a very embryonic stage of development. The thousand days of our youngest President had just begun, with their promise of excitement, possibility, greatness, and "a new frontier." But all of this optimism, hope, and good feeling about the future came to a crashing halt when those bullets rang out in Dallas on November 22, 1963. No corner of society was immune from the feelings of helplessness and despair triggered by the assassination of John Fitzgerald Kennedy.

Then came the Beatles.

BEATLEMANIA
AND THE
BRITISH INVASION

THE BEATLES

*Now, yesterday and today our theater's been jammed
with newspapermen and hundreds of photographers
from all over the nation, and these veterans agree with
me that the city has never seen the excitement stirred by
these youngsters from Liverpool who call themselves the
Beatles. Now, tonight you're going to be twice entertained by them. Right now, and again in the second half
of our show . . . ladies and gentlemen, the Beatles!*

With those words, on February 9, 1964, Ed Sullivan ushered in
a brand-new era of rock 'n' roll. In the depressing aftermath of
J.F.K.'s death, the world, particularly the United States, was

Ed Sullivan welcomes the Beatles—Ringo Starr, George Harrison, John Lennon, Paul McCartney.

looking for some kind of positive jolt that could lift it out of its collective doldrums, or at the very least distract it from the all-encompassing gloom of that still-unimaginable horror.

The jolt came, wonderfully enough, from "those four lovable moptops from Liverpool"—the Beatles. Or at least that's how they were described in the first, full tidal wave of Beatlemania that engulfed the globe in early 1964. If, as it is said, timing is everything, then the Beatles' punctuality was impeccable. Their arrival on the international stage simply could not have come at a better time. And it wasn't just their music, either. It was the way they looked. It was the way they dressed. It was what they said. And it was the *way* they said what they said.

The Beatles were more than Elvis times four. They captured the imagination and uplifted the human spirit more spectacularly than any other single entity in the history of mass entertainment. With their musical gifts, engaging manner, sharp wit, and delightful sense of humor, the Beatles' myth and stature grew to larger and larger proportions throughout the sixties.

It seemed at the time that they knew exactly what they were doing. It was only later on that we found out that they were making it up as they went along. Who would have thought that a bunch of Europeans could show America a thing or two about rock 'n' roll? But maybe we got careless with this great natural resource. Maybe we took it a little too much for granted, and allowed it to become somewhat diluted. The Beatles and their peers during the British Invasion, on the other hand, revered, digested, and assimilated the best of American rock 'n' roll, then hurled it back at us in refreshing, delightful new ways. How this all came about is a classic story, one unlikely to be eclipsed in our lifetimes.

When John Lennon met Paul McCartney in the mid-fifties, they were both hopelessly hooked on the music of American rock 'n' roll pioneers such as Elvis Presley, Chuck Berry, Carl Perkins, Little Richard, and Buddy Holly. Lennon had a skiffle group called the Quarrymen. He invited McCartney to join and the two were soon feverishly writing songs together. By the end of 1957, George Harrison had come aboard as lead guitarist, and the next year, Stu Sutcliffe, a school chum of Lennon's, became their bassist. Finally, in August 1960, Pete Best was added on drums.

Meanwhile, the name changed from the Quarrymen to Johnny and the Moondogs to the Silver Beatles—and ultimately, to just the Beatles. This basic unit paid their dues in the clubs and beerhalls of Liverpool and Hamburg, Germany. In April 1961, Stu Sutcliffe left the group to become a painter. (He died the following year from a brain hemorrhage.) The group continued as a quartet, with McCartney moving over to bass from rhythm guitar. By this time, the Beatles were playing to overflow crowds at the Cavern in Liverpool and doing backup vocals on records for British vocalist Tony Sheridan—one of which was a rock 'n' roll version of "My Bonnie"—as the Beat Boys.

On Saturday, October 28, 1961, a young teenager walked into a record store in Liverpool owned by the Epstein family and asked for a copy of "My Bonnie" by the Beatles. Brian Epstein was intrigued enough to go see the group perform live at the Cavern, and to subsequently offer his services as their manager.

On New Year's Day, 1962, the group traveled to London to audition for Decca Records. They were turned down. According to his own reminiscence, *A Cellarful of Noise,* Epstein responded, "You must be out of your mind. These boys are going to explode. I am completely confident that one day they will be bigger than Elvis Presley."

Apocryphal or not, the basic sentiment was destined to come true. In June 1962 the Beatles auditioned for producer George Martin, who signed them to a contract with EMI's Parlophone label. In August 1962 Pete Best was replaced on drums by Ringo Starr, who was from another popular Liverpool band, Rory Storm and the Hurricanes. On September 11, they cut "Love Me Do," and the temptation is to say that the rest is history.

Popular in England and parts of Europe throughout 1963, the Beatles did not make their move on America until 1964 during the post-Kennedy atmosphere described earlier. McCartney swore that this was all part of a well-thought-out plan in his 1980 interview with *Musician:*

> *The thing we did—which I always think new groups should take as a bit of advice—was that we were cheeky enough to say that we wouldn't go to the States until we had a number one record there. We were offered tours, but we knew we'd be second to someone and we didn't want that. There was a lot of careful thought behind it. There were a lot of artists who'd go over and vanish. . . . We always looked at it logically and thought, "Well, that's the mistake. You've got to go in as number one."*

And that is exactly what they did.

There was really no precedent for the success of the Beatles. It was all-encompassing. It touched so many people in so many ways at every level of society. The hits were a part of it. A lot of that early music was totally irresistible. But that was just the foundation. From that solid-rock base, the Beatle influence spilled over into many diverse areas.

Their films, for example, were startlingly fresh and original. *A Hard Day's Night* and *Help!* did much to enhance their legend and earn them the respect and admiration of an older audience. Their concert tours grew and grew in size and volume until it took baseball stadiums to contain them. The Beatles were welcome guests all over the world.

Their musical growth was equally astonishing. With each new single or album, they seemed to mature right before our eyes and ears. *Rubber Soul* and *Revolver,* in particular, displayed an unquenchable thirst to grow, expand, and create. Then, by 1966, the touring had become tiresome, and the group left the rigors of the road to concentrate on musical and artistic creativity. The end result in 1967 was the perfect album for that particular moment in our history.

Sgt. Pepper's Lonely Hearts Club Band defined the infamous Summer of Love and the rise of hippie culture and progressive rock that will be discussed in greater detail later on. Let it suffice to say that *Sgt. Pepper* hinted at heretofore unexplored possibilities for a rock 'n' roll album, and inspired a legion of fans and musicians in the process. Sounds exaggerated? Witness this excerpt from an essay by Langdon Winner in the book *Rock and Roll Will Stand:*

> *For the closest that Western civilization has come to unity since the Congress of Vienna in 1815 was the week that the* Sgt. Pepper *album was released. In every city in Europe and America the stereo systems and radios*

played [Sgt. Pepper] *and everyone listened. At the time I happened to be driving across country on Interstate 80. In each city where I stopped . . . the melodies wafted in from some far-off transistor radio or portable hi-fi. It was the most amazing thing I've ever heard. For a brief while the irreparably fragmented consciousness of the West was reunified, at least in the minds of the young. Every person listened to the record, pondered it, and discussed it with friends. While it is no doubt true that I have little in common with the gas station attendant in Cheyenne, Wyoming, we were able to come together to talk about the meaning of "A Day in the Life" during those few moments in which the oil in my VW was being changed.*

Such was the impact of the Beatles and rock 'n' roll in 1967. But no phenomenon is immune to pressures or changes—not even the Beatles. In fact, in some ways it's hard to imagine how they kept up their energy and output for as long as they did. Inevitably, the stress and strain of it all took a toll. One sign of it came in 1966. John Lennon did an interview with the *London Evening Standard* in which he offhandedly remarked that the Beatles were more popular than Jesus. He meant it as an example of how the world's values were out of whack, but when the interview was reprinted in an American teen magazine, the quote was taken out of context and caused an uproar. The Beatles spent a great deal of time on their 1966 U.S. tour explaining the quote and defending themselves. Then, in 1967, the death of Brian Epstein left the group without its chief strategist.

They could always regroup and somehow muster the energy

and creativity to put together wonderful collections of music—
such as *The Beatles*, usually called the "White Album," in 1968
and *Abbey Road* in 1969—but by 1970 the evidence was everywhere that the Beatles as a group had had it. John's divorce and
remarriage to Yoko Ono was a part of it. Paul's marriage to

The Beatles'
style after
Sgt. Pepper.

Linda Eastman was a part of it. So was George's need to express
himself, and Ringo's tiredness with the whole idea of being a
"Beatle." In April 1970 Paul McCartney made it official: The
Beatles were over.

John, Paul, George, and Ringo launched solo careers in the early seventies that enjoyed different kinds and degrees of success.

Ringo Starr had a couple of hit singles and albums in the seventies. He played on sessions with many notable rock 'n' roll stars, including solo projects for all three of his former bandmates. These days, Ringo is without a record deal and primarily active in films and television, but still loved and revered for his days as a Beatle.

George Harrison began his solo career with an explosion of musical activity, most notably the *All Things Must Pass* album and the Concert for Bangladesh. As the decade wore on, however, he became less and less active as a musician and performer. Today he is best known for his work as a film producer, including *Time Bandits* and *Shanghai Surprise*.

Paul McCartney has been the most consistently successful of all the ex-Beatles. Initially, he formed a second very popular band called Wings, which included his wife Linda and Denny Laine, formerly of the Moody Blues, among its members. Solo since 1980, Paul McCartney remains a gifted writer and engaging performer who can still whip together hugely entertaining singles and albums, seemingly at will. According to *The Guinness Book of World Records*, he is the most successful songwriter in music history.

Obviously, the saddest post-Beatle tale to tell is the story of John Lennon. His early solo work was wildly erratic and emotional, but it did include classics such as "Give Peace a Chance," "Imagine," "Mind Games," and "Whatever Gets You Thru the Night" (with back-up vocals by Elton John). He spent much of the early seventies campaigning for peace and fighting deportation from the United States over a minor drug conviction in England in the sixties. The deportation order was overturned on

October 7, 1975. Two days later, Yoko Ono gave birth to their son Sean, and John virtually retired from public life to become a househusband. In the fall of 1980, he returned to music with the album *Double Fantasy.* Half the songs were by John, half by Yoko. The music was mature, accomplished, and reflective—the work of a man obviously at peace with himself and his life. John Lennon was ready to reclaim his rightful place in the rock 'n' roll hierarchy.

Then, on December 8, 1980, as he returned from a mixing session for a new album, John was shot and killed by a deranged fan in the courtyard of the Dakota, the apartment building where he lived in New York City. A measure of the impact that the Beatles had on the world and on all of our lives is the fact that former anchorman Walter Cronkite began his broadcast of "The CBS Evening News" on December 9, 1980, with the following words:

> *The death of a man who sang and played guitar overshadows the news from Poland, Iran, and Washington tonight.*

John's murder forever put to rest the long-held hopes and dreams for a Beatles reunion. But chronicling their history and assessing their impact is an ongoing process. Their music continues to be immensely popular to old and new music fans alike. Many of the songs are established classics, regardless of musical genre. The Beatle legend continues to have a life of its own. It is the standard by which every fad and phenomenon must be measured. Spurred on by the temper of the times, the Beatles achieved dizzying heights of musical creativity, but it didn't just stop there. Without seeking it or even wanting it, they were handed leadership of the cultural explosion of the sixties. Then, without even trying, they created expectations that seemed impossible to live up to, then routinely surpassed them. That cultural impact remains unchallenged. No one has come close to it. Some may sell more records, and others may fill more concert halls, but the Beatles remain in a class by themselves. They are, quite simply, the most important group in the history of rock 'n' roll.

THE BRITISH INVASION

On the coattails of the Beatles came the British Invasion. Just about anyone with an English accent was fair game for American record companies. The trend was unmistakable. If the Beatles could be so well received, then certainly there were other young Englishmen who could capitalize on their breakthrough. Groups with established track records were ripe for the picking, and American radio, which had been revitalized by the success of the Beatles, was very receptive to the new English sounds.

In retrospect, it seems to me that there were three kinds of British Invasion bands: the dashers, the sprinters, and the long-distance runners. The dashers include all of those wonderful one-, two-, or three-hit wonders who captured the spotlight very quickly and then let go of it just as quickly—groups such as the Honeycombs ("Have I the Right"), Freddie and the Dreamers ("I'm Telling You Now"), Billy J. Kramer and the Dakotas ("Bad to Me," "Little Children"), and the Zombies ("She's Not There," "Tell Her No").

Then there are the sprinters who put together an impressive

The Dave Clark Five:
Mike Smith, Lenny Davidson,
Dennis Payton, Rick Huxley, Dave Clark.

body of work over the course of a few years, and then disappeared, disbanded, or went on to other pursuits. Here we would have to include some remarkable bands such as the Dave Clark Five ("Glad All Over," "Because," "Bits and Pieces," "Over and Over"), Herman's Hermits ("Mrs. Brown, You've Got a Lovely Daughter," "I'm Henry VIII, I Am," "Listen People," "There's a Kind of a Hush"), Gerry and the Pacemakers ("Don't Let the Sun Catch You Crying," "I Like It," "Ferry Cross the Mersey"), and the Animals ("The House of the Rising Sun," "Don't Let Me Be Misunderstood," "We Gotta Get Out of This Place," "It's My Life," "Don't Bring Me Down").

Somewhere between the sprinters and the long-distance runners, a special category must be created for the Hollies. Formed in Manchester, England, in 1962, the group centered around childhood friends Allan Clarke and Graham Nash. Named in tribute to the late Buddy Holly, the group typically earned early recognition in their homeland for cover versions of American pop and R&B hits. Success came a lot slower in the United States, but once the group cracked the American Top 10 in 1966 with "Bus Stop," the hits just kept on coming. Graham Nash quit the group in late 1968 after a dispute over musical direction. He

The Hollies: Allan Clarke, Bobby Elliott, Graham Nash, Bernie Calvert, Tony Hicks.

moved to America where, it turned out, even greater success awaited him. The Hollies continued to make hit records well into the seventies ("He Ain't Heavy . . . He's My Brother," "Long Cool Woman," "The Air That I Breathe"), and remained a consistently popular touring attraction. In 1983 Graham Nash reteamed with Allan Clarke, Tony Hicks, and Bobby Elliott for an album and a tour that only reaffirmed what rock fans knew all along: The Hollies were one of the most endearing and enduring bands of the British Invasion.

Finally, there are the long-distance runners—those precious few bands who may have been born in the shadow of the Beatles, but managed not only to outlast them but also, in the process, to make a lasting and significant impression on the history and direction of rock 'n' roll.

The Rolling Stones

First on this list would have to be the Rolling Stones, who have defied all of the oddsmakers and prognosticators, and now, well into their third decade together, can still legitimately lay claim to the title: World's Greatest Rock 'n' Roll Band.

In the early days of the British Invasion, the Stones played devil's advocate to the sainted Beatles. Their brand of rock 'n' roll was always a bit blacker, a bit bluer than the Fab Four, and had more of a jagged edge to it.

Mick Jagger and Keith Richards knew one another from childhood in Dartford, England, and began performing together sometime around 1960. Brian Jones from Cheltenham had played for a while with Alexis Korner's Blues Inc. (as did Mick Jagger). What these three shared in common (with an extraordi-

Early Stones:
Bill Wyman,
Brian Jones,
Mick Jagger,
Charlie Watts,
Keith Richards.

nary number of young white Englishmen, it turned out) was a deep, abiding passion for American blues and R&B. They began working together early in 1962 as the Rolling Stones—named after a Muddy Waters song. They debuted at London's Marquee Club on July 12. Following some personnel adjustments, which saw the addition of Bill Wyman on bass and Charlie Watts, who also played in Blues Inc., the Stones began a successful long-term engagement at the Crawdaddy Club. They released their first single—a cover version of Chuck Berry's "Come On"—in

June 1963. It did well enough to require a follow-up, which turned out to be Lennon and McCartney's "I Wanna Be Your Man," the only song recorded by both the Beatles and the Rolling Stones.

By early 1964, the group was a sensation in Britain, and, following the lead of the Beatles, made their first tour of the United States. Success in America came a little more slowly. Their first few singles here only made it to the lower end of the charts. But their tours, television appearances, and "bad boy" publicity paved the way for greater acceptance to come. It was precisely that publicity that gave the Stones their distinctive persona: surly, unkempt, uncooperative. The group cultivated that image, encouraged it, and went to great lengths to project and protect it. Their early press was not so much about their music as it was about their looks, behavior, and attitude.

Deserved or not, the image served them well. And so did the music. In the beginning, the Stones were totally derivative—steeped in the mighty Chicago blues tradition. They did uncanny covers of Chuck Berry, Muddy Waters, Bo Diddley, and Willie Dixon, as well as copycat originals in that style. And so it went until late 1964, when something happened. The Jagger–Richards songwriting team hit its stride with "Time Is on My Side," "Heart of Stone," and "The Last Time." That fact, coupled with the implacable musical experimentation of Brian Jones, and anchored by the rock-solid Wyman–Watts rhythm section, gave the Stones a completely unique identity, resulting in some of the most original and important rock 'n' roll of the sixties, the seventies, and the eighties.

Beginning with "(I Can't Get No) Satisfaction" in the summer of 1965, the Stones just kept on going and growing. Caught up in the creative maelstrom of the sixties, competitive to a fault with the Beatles (witness *Their Satanic Majesties Request*, their critically lambasted response to *Sgt. Pepper*), the Stones nonetheless produced a remarkable body of work between 1965 and 1969. The musical highs were matched by some well-documented personal lows: notorious drug busts, the resignation of Brian Jones from the band in June 1969 and his subsequent death by drowning less than a month later, and, perhaps worst of all, Altamont.

The Altamont Festival occurred at the end of a long and spectacularly successful tour of the United States in the late autumn of 1969. For the record, opening acts on the tour included English guitarist Terry Reid, B. B. King, Ike and Tina Turner, and Chuck Berry. The Stones were so pleased with the way things went that they decided to do a free concert for their fans as a way of saying thank you. The location chosen for the event was a huge stock-car oval called Altamont, fifty miles east of Berkeley, California. The arrangements were decided on, the appropriate announcements were made, and 300,000 rock fans showed up on December 6 with visions of a dream concert dancing in their heads.

But the dream turned into a nightmare when members of the infamous Hell's Angels Motorcycle Club were chosen as security guards for the occasion. The good intentions of the day were completely undone by a series of random acts of violence, culminating in the stabbing death of one concertgoer by a Hell's Angel. The entire event, including the murder, was captured on film by Albert and David Maysles for their documentary *Gimme Shelter*. All these many years later, the film contains a valuable lesson for anyone who ascribes too much power to their rock 'n' roll heroes, or thinks they are invulnerable. During the worst moments of violence (ironically, while the Stones were trying to play "Sympathy for the Devil"), Jagger attempts to restore some semblance of order to the proceedings. He fails miserably, and the chaos continues. Suddenly, in the course of a few frames of celluloid, he is no longer the omnipotent, larger-than-life rock star. Instead, we glimpse a frail, almost totally helpless mortal attempting in vain to deal with a horrendous circumstance at least partly of his own making, yet well beyond his control. The dark side of the power inherent in rock 'n' roll.

The tragedy at Altamont might have almost certainly dismantled a lesser group, but not so the Stones. In fact, as the new decade dawned, the Beatles were winding down, but the Stones were just catching their second wind. Freed by default from the competition with their Liverpool rivals, the Stones were liberated, rejuvenated—totally in a class by themselves. Yes, there was turmoil. There always will be with this group. Apparently, it is an essential ingredient of their success. Guitarist Mick Taylor, who had replaced Brian Jones, left the band in 1974. He was replaced—temporarily at first, then permanently—by Ron Wood. Keith Richards's alternating problems with drugs and the law placed the group's future in jeopardy on more than one occasion. But so far the band has always managed to overcome any and all obstacles placed in its path, and to come back bigger and stronger than ever as the situation demanded. And there is always a ready and waiting audience for whatever it is the Stones choose to do. Amazingly, in this fickle world, they have held on to their old fans from the early days and just keep adding new ones.

There are very good reasons for this, of course. First and foremost, there is the music—a still-gutsy, guitar-based, blues-drenched raunch and roll that is uniquely their own. Then there is the legendary Mick Jagger persona—the pouting, prancing, posturing prototype for every young vocalist who dares to dream about becoming lead singer in a rock 'n' roll band. Finally, they are more defiant now in middle age than they were as young adults, albeit in different ways. They refuse to lie down, roll over, and play dead for whatever the new fad, phase, or "phenom" of rock 'n' roll may be. Instead, they just keep churning out memorable singles, worthy albums, and incredible tours that remind people exactly how vital and important rock 'n' roll has become in our lives. Just listen to selected songs from various checkpoints throughout their career: "Satisfaction" in 1965; "Jumpin' Jack Flash" in 1968; "Honky Tonk Women" in 1969; "Brown Sugar" in 1971; "It's Only Rock 'n' Roll" in 1974; "Miss You" in 1978; or "Start Me Up" in 1981. These milestones are inextricably linked to the absolute best that rock 'n' roll can be. Charlie Watts once marveled in an interview at the continuing vitality and energy of musicians from the Big Band era who still make vital and vibrant music well into their sixties and seventies, often with their original bandmates. If their 1986 album, *Dirty Work*, is any indication, I'm betting the Stones will do likewise. It may only be rock 'n' roll, but apparently they like it—very, very much.

The Kinks

The term "rock 'n' roll survivor" can have many different meanings. It applies to everything from a fifties rock star who is still recording and performing to a fan who grows from child to adult with his or her love for rock 'n' roll intact. But the term has a truly special meaning when applied to the Kinks.

The Kinks exploded onto the music scene in late 1964 at the height of the British Invasion. Their early recordings literally screamed for attention. Their music was louder, cruder, and more compelling than just about anything anyone else was doing in Britain or the States. The central reasons for this were two brothers from London named Ray and Dave Davies. Ray was an art college student when he joined his brother's band in the early sixties. Typically, the group did cover versions of American rock hits such as "Long Tall Sally" and "Louie, Louie" and monosyllablic originals of their own, such as "All Day and All of the Night." But soon after their initial success, the Kinks began to exhibit equal skill with softer, more subtle examinations of British life and hypocrisies in songs along the lines of "A Well Respected Man" and "Dedicated Follower of Fashion." Credit for this latter development must go largely to the group's main songwriter and natural leader: Ray Davies.

In a discussion about "A Well Respected Man," a scathing indictment of the British upper class, Ray told me in 1977: "I just wrote the song as a joke, really, and we recorded it, and it was a hit in America as a single, and a fatal thing happened to me. I discovered words. And even worse, I got a dictionary. Then you go into another facet. It's another world."

And what a world it was! A world of rock operas (*Victoria, or the Decline and Fall of the British Empire* in 1969), and stunning concept albums (*Preservation Act I* in 1973, *Preservation Act II* in 1974, and *Soap Opera* in 1975, to name a few). Davies

The Kinks
(clockwise from
top left):
Ray Davies,
Mick Avory,
Dave Davies,
Peter Quaife.

became the unofficial poet laureate of the working class. With occasional exceptions like "Lola" in 1970, the drift toward artier rock 'n' roll cost the group their Top 40 successes, but they were embraced by critics and diehard fans alike.

For most of the seventies, the Kinks acquired a reputation for their wildly erratic, drunken stage shows that often culminated in loud onstage arguments between the volatile Davies brothers. In the late seventies, when the musical tides began to shift dramatically away from the more ornate and conceptual kind of rock to a cruder, more basic style, the Kinks abandoned concept albums and opted again for pared-down, crisply produced collections of rock songs that once again yielded hit singles, such as "A Rock 'n' Roll Fantasy," "Sleepwalker," and "Superman."

Meanwhile, a new generation of young bands was rediscovering or realizing for the first time that the Kinks were punk all along. Van Halen had a hit with "You Really Got Me." The Pretenders resurrected "Stop Your Sobbing." All of a sudden, the Kinks were big time once more—playing arenas, placing hit singles such as "Come Dancing" on the charts, and making imaginative videos. Through all of their stylistic changes, personnel changes, and attitude changes, Ray and Dave Davies remain at the core, giving the group its stability and artistic tension. True rock 'n' roll survivors—the Kinks Kronikle Kontinues!

The Who

Writing about the Who fills me with mixed emotions—celebrating their triumphs, commiserating with their tragedies. I remember distinctly receiving their first American single, "I Can't Explain," at my college radio station in early 1965. It was thrilling and delightful, but went nowhere commercially. Nor did subsequent releases such as "My Generation," "Substitute," and "The Kids Are Alright." It was hard to believe. Here was a group making angry, volatile rock 'n' roll records—already big stars in their own country—yet they were all but ignored in the U.S.

It made no sense. The Who was the perfect four-piece rock combo: Roger Daltrey's impassioned vocals, John Entwistle's stone-faced bass playing, Keith Moon's maniacal drum thrashing and trashing, Pete Townshend's windmill guitar playing and prolific songwriting. The Who was a portable earthquake, with their fans gleefully registering each new mighty tremor.

Success in the United States finally came in 1967. First of all, their infectious single "Happy Jack" made it to number twenty-four on the charts. Second, on a cross-country tour opening for the perennial British hit makers Herman's Hermits, the Who stole the show with their powerful stage act that ended with Townshend violently smashing his guitar to bits and Moon kicking over his drum kit. This attention-getting device served two purposes. It generated lots and lots of publicity, and it came to symbolize not only the violence in our global society, but also the fury contained in a great deal of late sixties rock 'n' roll that was aimed at an old, familiar target—the Establishment.

It wasn't just their hit singles and dynamic concert performances that began winning over large numbers of fans. As far back as their second album, the Who was experimenting with very progressive, long form recordings that stretched the outer limits of rock, and challenged their peers and successors to greater and greater levels of accomplishment. With the release of

The Who onstage:
John Entwistle,
Roger Daltrey,
Keith Moon,
Pete Townshend.

Townshend's rock opera *Tommy* in 1969, the Who became a true mass phenomena. Seeing them at New York's Metropolitan Opera House in June 1970 performing *Tommy* in its entirety in an incredibly sophisticated and symbolic environment was a perfect statement about how far rock 'n' roll had come in just fifteen years.

The Who continued their leadership role well into the seventies, but two tragedies sealed the group's fate. On September 7,

1978, Keith Moon succumbed to an overdose of a sedative he was taking to curb his alcoholism. The surviving band members regrouped, added British rock veteran Kenney Jones on drums, and valiantly attempted to continue on, but, as might be expected, the Who was a different band without Keith Moon.

Then, in December 1979, eleven concertgoers were trampled to death in a mad rush for seats at a Who concert at Riverfront Stadium in Cincinnati. In a way, it was the last straw. A new album followed in 1981, and another in 1982, but the end was near. In 1982 the group announced their farewell tour of North America. The final performance took place on December 17, 1982, in Toronto, Canada. And while there certainly will be continuing solo efforts by the group's individual members (Townshend's "White City" and Daltrey's "Under a Raging Moon" in 1985), and maybe even an occasional, rare reunion for charitable purposes (Live Aid), one unforgettable, irreplaceable era in rock 'n' roll history had come to an end.

AMERICA'S
RESPONSE
TO THE
BRITISH INVASION

The Beatles and their peers had a devastating double-edged impact on American radio and record companies. On the one hand, they revitalized slumping record sales and stale radio formats. On the other hand, few old-line rock 'n' rollers were able to compete with the British onslaught. There were notable exceptions, of course, such as the Beach Boys and the Four Seasons, but in a very real and unprecedented way, the pioneers of this uniquely American form were supplanted by outsiders. Slowly but surely, American musicians rebounded. They adapted and reassimilated what was theirs to begin with—rock 'n' roll.

In addition, a new generation of young people who were raised on rock 'n' roll, inspired by the Beatles, and influenced by every conceivable strain of music started infiltrating the ranks of the American music business. Eager to take part in the pop explosion of the sixties, they began writing their own songs, arranging them, forming their own groups to perform them— some of the more adventurous even made forays into the studio to record them. The end result was a tremendous infusion of new blood into the music business and an incredibly exciting time for American rock 'n' roll.

SOUL MUSIC

The resurgence took place simultaneously on many fronts. One of the most important was the American record buyers' continuing fascination with black music. Just as in the earliest days of rock 'n' roll, music fans embraced rhythm and blues in all of its varied forms from roots rock 'n' roll to Motown to "blue-eyed soul"—the term used to describe white musicians who did credible facsimiles of black music. (Most notable in the sixties were the Righteous Brothers and the Young Rascals. At this writing, the reigning champions of blue-eyed soul are Hall and Oates.)

Even a random glance at the American music charts for any week of the post-Beatle sixties is sure to reveal an R&B treasure nestled in among the "British biscuits." Lots of Motown, of course. In addition to the groups and individuals already profiled, there were chart successes by Mary Wells and Jr. Walker and the All Stars. And beyond the Motor City, there were plenty of solid black hits and artists from every corner of the music spectrum. Betty Everett, Louis Armstrong, Ray Charles, Dionne Warwick, the Drifters, Bobby Freeman, Jerry Butler, Little Anthony and the Imperials, Shirley Ellis, Sam Cooke, and

The late Sam Cooke was a gospel singer turned pop star who helped define soul music in the late fifties and early sixties.

Joe Tex all had Top 10 singles within a year of the Beatles' first appearance on the U.S. surveys.

As the decade and the civil rights struggle raged on, a veritable Who's Who of American black music started with greater and greater frequency to cross over from the strictly rhythm and blues charts to the more mainstream Top 40. Again, in addition to the mighty Motown roster, this was the period that saw the emergence of stars such as Wilson Pickett, Ramsey Lewis, Curtis Mayfield (with and without the Impressions), Otis Redding, Percy Sledge, Sam and Dave, Bobby Hebb—and at least three artists whose success and impact is as great today as it was back at the beginning of their long and influential careers, namely James Brown, Aretha Franklin, and Tina Turner.

James Brown, the Godfather of Soul, actually recorded his first R&B hits in the fifties but it wasn't until 1965 that he crossed over to the American Top 10 with a string of hits, such as "Papa's Got a Brand New Bag," "I Got You (I Feel Good)," "It's a Man's Man's Man's World," and "I Got the Feelin'." After a slump in his career in the seventies, James Brown came back bigger and better than ever in the eighties. He appeared in *The Blues Brothers* movie and had a Top 10 hit with his song from *Rocky IV*, "Living in America."

Similarly, the Queen of Soul—Aretha Franklin—enjoyed her greatest success in the sixties with "Respect," "Chain of Fools," and "(You Make Me Feel Like) A Natural Woman." Personal problems kept her inactive for most of the late seventies, but in 1985 her album *Who's Zoomin' Who* produced a number of smash singles, including the title track and "Freeway of Love."

Finally, Tina Turner began her recording career with former

The hardest-working man in show business— James Brown (right).

husband Ike in 1960. Their first hit single was "It's Gonna Work Out Fine" in 1961. The Ike and Tina Turner live revue became a major soul act in the United States, producing occasional chart singles as well, the most successful of which was their remake of "Proud Mary" in 1971. Following a bitter divorce in the mid-seventies, Tina's career languished on the oldies circuit for a while. Opening shows for the Stones and Rod Stewart helped to keep her in the public eye. Then, in 1984, she staged a dramatic comeback with the platinum album *Private Dancer*, which included the number one hit single "What's Love Got to Do with It." She is one of the biggest female solo stars of the eighties.

FOLK ROCK

Another major American offensive against the British Invasion—which in turn had a corresponding impact on English musicians—was the whole folk rock phenomenon.

Folk rock is the very simple and accurate term used to describe the marriage of traditional folk music and American rock 'n' roll that took place on a very large scale in the mid-sixties. What rock liked about folk was the lyrical depth, the musical textures, and the emotional intensity. What folk liked about rock was the electricity (literally and figuratively), the sense of excitement and fun, and the direct access to a ready and waiting mass audience. In fact, folk rock provided the means to make powerful statements and send meaningful messages to a larger audience than had ever before been possible for each form separately.

Folk music in and of itself is a treasure trove of diversity: everything from English and Scottish ballads to black spirituals and work songs. It thrived for centuries in every corner of the globe and made the trip to the New World with every boatload of settlers from all over the world. Once here, the process continued, becoming even richer by virtue of the greater variety of influences that intermingled throughout North America. With the advent of recording and broadcast technology, folk music achieved even speedier cross-pollination, along with wider exposure, than ever before. And a very distinctive kind of American folk performer began to emerge. These men and women were not so much musicians as they were journalists—eyewitnesses to history who used guitars and phonograph records the way most reporters used typewriters and printing presses. They wrote about events. They wrote about issues. They wrote about their feelings on poverty and injustice. They expressed complicated thoughts in simple structures.

The prototypical American folksinger was Woody Guthrie. He was born on July 14, 1912, in Okemah, Oklahoma. He left home as a teenager, traveling around the country, working at various odd jobs, and writing songs—always writing songs. During the Depression, Woody continued to incorporate observations about things he'd seen and people he'd met into his music while riding the rails across the country. His writing became more and more political, and he used the American folk ballad as a form for protest and social comment. In the early forties he joined the Almanac Singers with Pete Seeger and Lee Hays, appearing at union meetings and political rallies. In the early fifties, Guthrie was diagnosed as having Huntington's chorea, a genetically transmitted debilitating disease. Eventually, he was hospitalized and bedridden until his death in October 1967.

Meanwhile, in 1949, Pete Seeger and Lee Hays, together with Ronnie Gilbert and Fred Hellerman, formed the Weavers, probably the single most influential folk quartet in American popular music. They took folk music to the national popularity charts with a string of hit records throughout the fifties, including the traditional folk ballad "On Top of Old Smokey," Leadbelly's "Goodnight, Irene," and Woody Guthrie's "So Long, It's Been Good to Know You." Because of their leftist leanings, the group had problems with blacklisting during the McCarthy era. They split up and reunited a couple of times until Seeger left the group in 1958 to go solo. The original members got together for a reunion concert at New York's Carnegie Hall on November 28, 1980. The event was documented in the very moving and affecting film *Wasn't That a Time*. Lee Hays died on August 26, 1981. But it is quite clear that, along with Woody Guthrie, the Weavers were directly and primarily responsible for the Great American Folk Revival of the late fifties and early sixties that saw a tremendous explosion of young talent, including the Kingston Trio; the Highwaymen; the Limelighters; the Serendipity Singers; Peter, Paul, and Mary; Joan Baez; Judy Collins; Dave Van Ronk; Tom Paxton; Eric Andersen; and Phil Ochs.

And, in a category by himself, there was Bob Dylan.

Bob Dylan

Bob Dylan was born Robert Allen Zimmerman in Duluth, Minnesota, on May 24, 1941. When he was six years old, he moved with his family to Hibbing, Minnesota, and gradually became influenced by a great variety of musical styles and artists. He learned to play guitar and harmonica and began performing while in high school. After enrolling at the University of Minnesota in 1959, he started doing solo performances at local coffeehouses under the name Bob Dylan (apparently after the Welsh poet Dylan Thomas). By this time, he was a serious student of American folk music, borrowing liberally from originals such as Woody Guthrie and Ramblin' Jack Elliott.

He quit college after a couple of semesters and moved to New York City in January 1961, on a pilgrimage to meet Woody Guthrie. He frequently visited his idol at Greystone Park Hospital in New Jersey, and the two became friends. Soon Dylan was swapping songs and stories with Guthrie cronies such as Seeger and Dave Van Ronk. He made his first professional appearance at Gerdes Folk City in New York's Greenwich Village on April 11, 1961. After a rave review by music critic Robert Shelton in *The New York Times* on September 29, Dylan was signed by producer John Hammond at Columbia Records to a recording contract. (Hammond also signed Aretha Franklin and Bruce Springsteen, among others.)

With his scruffy appearance and, to put it mildly, unconventional singing voice, Dylan was snidely referred to in the hallways of CBS as "Hammond's Folly." But in this case, the artist and his mentor definitely had the last laugh. His first album in 1962, *Bob Dylan*, was largely derivative, containing faithful versions of traditional folk and blues songs. But mixed in among the covers were two originals—"Talkin' New York" and "Song to Woody"—the former a wry and funny account of young Bob's early experiences in the Big Apple, done to perfection in Woody Guthrie's talking blues style, and the latter an out-and-out tribute to his folk heroes—mainly Woody. But, even as he was

Bob Dylan—
the voice of a
generation.

heaping praise on his idols, he was also, in a sense, leaving them behind. He had his own roads to wander and trails to blaze.

By his second album, *The Freewheelin' Bob Dylan*, he was prolifically writing songs of startling freshness and originality, unmatched by his peers or elders. This one record contains quintessential Dylan anthems such as "Blowin' in the Wind," "Masters of War," and "A Hard Rain's A-Gonna Fall." Somehow, some way, he forged his own style and found his own voice, relying less and less on the influence of others and more and more on his own instincts and passions. To the surprise of just about everyone, including himself, his became the voice of an entire generation. At first, he accomplished this largely through his songwriting. On the one hand, inflammatory protest material (he called them finger-pointing songs), on the other hand, intensely personal songs about love and relationships. And if his nasal, whining vocals seemed ill-suited to AM radio at the time, this was soon overcome by pleasing cover versions of his songs by early champions and supporters such as Joan Baez, Judy Collins, and especially Peter, Paul, and Mary, who took "Blowin' in the Wind" and "Don't Think Twice, It's Alright" to the top of the singles charts in 1963.

As if possessed by some divine muse, Dylan continued to write and sing songs that addressed and articulated the hopes and fears and dreams of an entire segment of the population. But soon the folk idiom seemed too narrow for him, too limiting. Sensing the dramatic shift of post-Beatles rock music to a more serious and meaningful content, Dylan slowly began introducing electric instruments in his recorded works and live appearances—to the chagrin of his purist folk fans and to the delight of a much larger mass audience than he could ever have reached with his strictly folk recordings.

Dylan produced three classic rock 'n' roll albums during this period—or, at the very least, three albums that contained and merged the best elements of folk and rock. First, in March 1965 there was *Bringing It All Back Home*, followed rapidly in August by *Highway 61 Revisited* (with his Top 40 breakthrough single, "Like a Rolling Stone"), and finally the two-record set *Blonde on Blonde* in May 1966.

It was during this period that Dylan began working with a back-up group called simply the Band. Rick Danko, Levon Helm, Garth Hudson, Richard Manuel, and Robbie Robertson emerged on their own in 1968 with the album *Music from Big Pink*. After that, with and without Bob Dylan, the Band continued to have a major impact on rock 'n' roll well into the seventies until their final performance together on Thanksgiving night, 1976. This momentous event with invited guests from every corner of the musical spectrum was documented in Martin Scorcese's critically acclaimed film *The Last Waltz*. Completely on their own, the Band earned a respected and well-deserved place in rock history for the vivid and haunting portraits of Americana in their music.

On July 29, 1966, at the absolute height of his rock 'n' roll powers and popularity, Bob Dylan was seriously injured in a motorcycle accident near his home in Woodstock, New York. His recovery was long and slow, and his withdrawal from the public was total. Whatever reevaluation of his life and his art that took place at this time has set the tone for all of the various Dylan personas we have seen periodically since then.

When he finally emerged from seclusion in January 1968, it was at a tribute to Woody Guthrie at Carnegie Hall. His album at the time, *John Wesley Harding,* marked a return to simplicity, far from the hard-rocking edge of its immediate predecessors. In 1969 he even adopted a brand-new singing voice for the pure country stylings of *Nashville Skyline.*

In the seventies, the record-buying public had several different Dylans to choose from, starting with the poorly received *Self-Portrait* album in 1970. It was a two-record set of mostly cover versions of other people's material. In 1974 he released the quintessential Bob Dylan album of the seventies, *Blood on the Tracks,* a mature, introspective look at love and relationships that was a major critical and commercial success. In 1975 he organized the Rolling Thunder Revue, a traveling rock 'n' roll communal tour with longtime friends and associates, including Joan Baez, Roger McGuinn, and Joni Mitchell. In 1979, Dylan became a born-again Christian and released the openly spiritual album *Slow Train Coming.*

He continued in this latter vein early in the eighties on *Saved* and *Shot of Love,* then returned to a more conventional form of expression on *Infidels, Empire Burlesque,* and *Knocked Out Loaded.* These days there are even Bob Dylan videos to ponder and wonder about. But to expect familiarity and predictability from Bob Dylan is to completely miss the point. Well into his fifth decade, he remains one of the most consistently interesting and fascinating characters in American music.

Yet, amid all this adulation and accrued respect, there is a built-in trap. So much is demanded of him by so many that he couldn't possibly live up to people's expectations of him if he had three lifetimes to do it in. So he doesn't even try. His legacy is set firmly in place. It is impossible to predict the exact moment that he will next unleash a significant masterpiece on an unsuspecting world or write a song of such resonance and value that it eclipses whatever else is going on in popular music at the moment. He carries the baggage of his glorious past with him wherever he goes. Sometimes it gets in the way, but often it serves him well, particularly when he lends his artistic weight to a worthy cause like U.S.A. for Africa, Live Aid or Farm Aid.

He continues to mystify, outrage, satisfy, challenge, and enthrall audiences of many ages. It is impossible to ignore or escape his influence. It can be seen and heard in the work of so many diverse artists, male and female alike, all across the musical spectrum. Anyone who has been touched by the depth and breadth of his career has a favorite Dylan memory. Mine occurred on August 1, 1971, at New York's Madison Square Garden during the afternoon performance of George Harrison's Concert for Bangladesh. It was a truly star-studded event before a spellbound audience. Everyone's senses were totally immersed in the enjoyment of rock legends Harrison, Ringo Starr, Eric Clapton, Leon Russell, Billy Preston, and others. There had been rumors beforehand of other possible guests at the concert, but most of them centered around the possibility of a never-to-be Beatles reunion. So I, for one, was taken totally by surprise that afternoon when I noticed out of the corner of my eye a familiar, curly-haired, denim-clad figure with an acoustic guitar and harmonica making his way to center stage to begin an unannounced, unexpected performance. It was Dylan, of course, with a mesmerizing five-song set that dazzled the assembled multitude: "A

Hard Rain's A-Gonna Fall," "It Takes a Lot to Laugh," "Blowin' in the Wind," "Mr. Tambourine Man," and, with Harrison and Russell, "Just Like a Woman."

His appearance there that day crystallized for me several facts about Bob Dylan and rock 'n' roll. First of all, it was a coming together of rock royalty for a worthy cause, and in that gesture was contained the seeds which prefigured all of the wonderful charitable happenings that have occurred since. Second, I realized that the power and timelessness of Dylan's best songs are etched upon our consciousness and will not diminish no matter what the current trend or fad. He has the ability to reflect the concerns of a mass of people in an intimate, personal way, and the power to focus the attention of many on the plight of a few.

The universality of music as a healer and bonder, even as it riles and instigates, was overwhelmingly evident that August afternoon. It was an event that was destined to rank among the greatest moments in all of rock 'n' roll history, and to serve as a milestone and inspiration for all such future exhibitions of rock's heart, soul, and generosity. And so it has.

In one of those serendipitous coincidences that seemed to be commonplace in the music scene of the sixties, while Dylan was busy embracing rock 'n' roll, rock 'n' roll with equal tenacity was embracing Bob Dylan. Groups of substance and significance, powered by pulsating drums and raging electric guitars (always with room for an occasional acoustic piece), plundered the Dylan song catalog searching with a fine-tooth comb for gems to transform into full-blown rock anthems. They found many.

• / / / •

The Folk Rock Bands

Major credit for this phenomenon must be given to the Byrds. Led by Chicago folkie Jim (later Roger) McGuinn, and also including David Crosby, Chris Hillman, Gene Clark, and Michael Clarke, this Los Angeles–based quintet took an electrified version of Dylan's "Mr. Tambourine Man" to the top of the charts in June 1965. They followed this accomplishment with a version of Pete Seeger's "Turn! Turn! Turn!" (from the Bible's Book of Ecclesiastes) that also went to number one. They also had successful singles with their own compositions "Eight Miles

Folk rock pioneers—the Byrds: Gene Clark, Roger McGuinn, Chris Hillman, David Crosby, Michael Clarke.

High," "Mr. Spaceman," and "So You Want to Be a Rock 'n' Roll Star," plus Dylan's "All I Really Want to Do" and "My Back Pages." Just as Peter, Paul, and Mary had made Dylan palatable for the mass folk audience, the Byrds paved the way for his emergence as a rock star in his own right. By October 1965, Dylan had placed two of his own songs, "Like a Rolling Stone" and "Positively 4th Street," in the American Top 10, and the mid-sixties folk rock boom was in full swing.

The Byrds, in varying configurations, continued as a major influence on rock 'n' roll into the seventies, exploring and experimenting with various musical styles, most notably country rock, but never straying too far from the readily familiar and identifiable sound of Roger McGuinn's distinctive lead vocals and soaring 12-string electric guitar.

Right behind the Byrds were a number of groups that deserve recognition for their contributions to folk rock. In no particular order, they are:

Bubbling up from the clubs and coffeehouses of New York's Greenwich Village, the Lovin' Spoonful (who took their name from a R&B lyric) fused folk, rock, and jug band music into a frothy blend of good-time rock 'n' roll that captured the hearts of music fans all across the country. Built around the songwriting talents of former New York session musician John Sebastian, the Lovin' Spoonful landed hit after hit on the pop surveys, such as "You Didn't Have to Be So Nice," "Daydream," and "Summer in the City." Sebastian departed for a solo career in 1968. "Do You Believe in Magic?" was the question they posed to a generation of mid-sixties rock fans, and the answer came back loud and clear— it was a resounding *"Yes!"*

Similarly oriented toward good-time rock, but with a West Coast rather than an East Coast perspective, were the Turtles. Starting out as a surf band called the Crossfires, the group embraced folk rock, changed their name, and had a Top 10 hit with Bob Dylan's "It Ain't Me, Babe" in August 1965. The group's sound was centered around lead vocalists Mark Volman and Howard Kaylan, who have maintained a personal friendship and professional partnership that has weathered every major shift and change in the direction of popular music over the last twenty years. They continue today as rock's premier parodists and leaders of the annual "Happy Together" tours—a traveling caravan of sixties hitmakers named after the Turtles' biggest hit, a number one single in 1967.

Two of the major faces and forces in rock 'n' roll for over two decades have been Stephen Stills and Neil Young. They, together with Richie Furay (who had performed with Stills in a New York folk group called the Au-Go-Go Singers), Bruce Palmer (a Canadian colleague of Young's), and Dewey Martin, formed the nucleus of a volatile, explosive, and creative ensemble known as the Buffalo Springfield. Formed after a chance encounter in Los Angeles in 1966, the group put together their various folk, rock, and country backgrounds into a very sophisticated, highly charged blend. They influenced major forces in rock 'n' roll of the seventies, such as the Eagles and Linda Ronstadt, and can still be heard today reverberating in the works of artists such as Jackson Browne and Dan Fogelberg. Their best-known songs include "For What It's Worth," "Sit Down, I Think I Love You," and "Bluebird."

• / / / •

The Mamas and
the Papas
(clockwise from
top right):
Cass Elliot,
Denny Doherty,
Michelle Phillips,
John Phillips.

One of the premier groups of the folk rock era, the Mamas and the Papas consisted of Denny Doherty, the late Cass Elliot, and John and Michelle Phillips. They got together in 1965 after discovering how exquisitely their four voices blended together. On the strength of John Phillips's prolific songwriting and accompanied in concert and on record by the best Los Angeles studio musicians, they placed hit after hit on the charts, beginning with "California Dreamin'" in February 1966, and continuing with "Monday Monday," "I Saw Her Again," "Words of Love," and "Creeque Alley"—a biographical song about many of the prime movers of American folk rock. Among the group's major accomplishments was the organization of the Monterey Pop Festival in June 1967—the prototypical late-sixties rock festival. Internal conflict and drug abuse put an end to the group in 1968, but their influence can certainly be heard in the seventies work of Fleetwood Mac and the eighties success of the Bangles.

Simon and Garfunkel

Special mention must be made of a folk rock duo from Queens, New York, who made a deep and lasting impression on the popular music landscape of the sixties and early seventies. The tall one on the left has bushy hair and the voice of an angel. The short one on the right appears intensely serious (though not without a redeeming sense of humor) and writes songs of enduring beauty and lyricism. Paul Simon and Art Garfunkel were neighborhood buddies and school chums who began performing together as early as the sixth grade in Forest Hills, New York. Completely taken by the rock 'n' roll of the late fifties, Art and Paul put a record called "Hey, Schoolgirl" on the charts in 1957 as Tom and Jerry. By the early sixties, the two were caught up in the folk boom of the time and, through the efforts of producer Tom Wilson, signed a recording contract with Columbia Records.

Wednesday Morning, 3 A.M., a purely acoustic folk album by Simon and Garfunkel, was released in mid-1964 and went nowhere. Paul took off to live and work in England, and Art went on to graduate school at Columbia University. Then, as a result of one of the more bizarre twists of fate in rock 'n' roll history, Simon and Garfunkel became major stars without even trying. Producer Tom Wilson, impressed by the impact of folk rock and certain that Simon and Garfunkel should be a part of it, took one of the best songs on their debut album and added an electric bass and drums to the basic tracks. The results were mesmerizing. "The Sounds of Silence" hit number one in December 1965 and launched the career of one of the most important duos in pop music history.

Throughout 1966 and 1967, Simon and Garfunkel continued their string of hit singles, popular albums, and sold-out concerts. Then, in 1968, as a result of their contributions to the soundtrack of the runaway hit motion picture *The Graduate,* coupled with a blockbuster new album called *Bookends,* Simon and Garfunkel ascended to rock stardom, dominating the albums and singles charts and filling concert halls and larger venues at will. They topped these achievements in 1970 with the release of *Bridge Over Troubled Water,* one of the most honored and popular albums in the history of recorded music. But soon after its release, they chose to go their separate ways and pursue solo careers.

Then, in the late summer of 1981, rumors were rampant about a possible Simon and Garfunkel reunion. The rumors became reality when Paul and Art did a free concert on September 19

Art Garfunkel and
Paul Simon in concert.

that was attended by approximately 400,000 fans of all ages in New York's Central Park. A recording of the event became a best-selling album, and a videotape of it sold well and continues to play on cable television. The reunion proved conclusively that the magic was still there for the asking. The best of their music speaks as eloquently today as it did when it was originally written and recorded. The love of their old fans was reaffirmed, even as new fans were discovering what the fuss was all about in the first place.

THE
LATE
SIXTIES

By the end of 1966, it was abundantly clear that rock 'n' roll was taking on a larger and larger significance in the lives of American young people, and, by extension, in the larger society as well. The civil rights movement, anti-Vietnam War sentiment, free speech, students' rights, the sexual revolution—all of these disparate causes found their anthems in the rhythms and rhetoric of rock. In the nineteenth century, the poet Walt Whitman had observed: "To have great poetry, you need a great audience." Well, sixties audiences routinely demanded greatness from their musicians, and, by and large, those musicians rose to the occasion. From the Beatles on down, rock 'n' roll whipped itself into a frenzy of creative experimentation. There were no limits. Anything was possible. Rock merged, fused, enmeshed itself with every conceivable form. If there could be folk rock, then surely there could be blues rock and classical rock and jazz rock and rock opera—on and on. And so there was. All practiced with great seriousness and even greater dedication by the best musicians of a generation.

It was a wonderful time to be coming of age in America. There were high expectations. There was a whole generation giddy with the realization of its own power and self-importance. There was great rock 'n' roll. And, for all too brief a period, there was progressive FM radio.

THE FLOWERING OF FM

FM was the often-maligned, misused brainchild of Major Edwin Armstrong, who committed suicide in 1954, largely out of frustration over the mistreatment of his invention. The progress of FM, with its superior sound quality and stereophonic capability, was hampered by entrepreneurs who had a vested interest in the development of television. Why confuse the public, they reasoned, or distract attention away from TV? And so, Armstrong's invention was ignored. Then, after years of languishing as a backup medium for the more successful and established AM radio transmission, FM got a new lease on life in 1965 when the Federal Communications Commission, besieged by requests for new radio stations, took a dramatic step. They decided that, in markets of a certain size, broadcasters could no longer air the same content on both their AM and FM stations, a practice known as simulcasting. (Today the term more commonly refers to the stereophonic broadcast by an FM station of the soundtrack of a particular television show.) The result was broad experimentation on the FM dial.

One of those bold experiments brought rock 'n' roll to FM. It was another simply smashing example of great timing. Post-Beatle rock had just about outgrown the time constraints and content restraints of AM radio, where hit singles had to be under three minutes long and totally noncontroversial. The lengthy song-poems of artists such as Bob Dylan and Arlo Guthrie were all but shut out. They found a ready and waiting home, however, on FM. These new stations, hungry for audiences and identities of their own, welcomed the new rock, its youthful creators, and the many new and innovative ways of presenting them.

These techniques included playing album cuts instead of Top 40 singles, arranging selections into sets of music organized around a particular theme, performer, or similarity of sound, and conducting lengthy and serious interviews with the artists making the music. And perhaps the most radical difference in the presentation of rock 'n' roll on FM could be found in the disc jockeys chosen to play it. In contrast to their AM counterparts, these men and (more and more as the years went on) women were soft-spoken, knowledgeable, and apparently committed to the philosophies behind the music.

Not surprisingly, this type of approach first surfaced on college campuses in the mid-sixties, where young people, touched to the core by the new rock, were beginning to influence the direction of their university radio stations. It spread quickly enough to commercial stations in the bigger cities—and with good reason. There was an audience out there clamoring for it. An audience hungry for the content and sense of community that these stations provided. Picture it: A young person who was being hassled by his parents about the length of his hair or the loudness of his music could go to his room, switch on the FM radio, and get instant reaffirmation of the things he believed in and cared about. And know that at that precise moment countless other listeners who felt exactly the same way about the world were sharing that sensation and those feelings.

Although termed "underground," FM rock radio was very much above ground—quite a visible tree in the nation's media forest, accessible with the mere flip of a radio dial. FM became a rallying point, a meeting place for listeners who shared similar attitudes about politics, war, peace, sex, and—maybe most important—rock 'n' roll. The disc jockeys (or radio personalities, as this group generally preferred to be called) seemed like hip allies against some common oppression. And the superior sound quality of FM ("no static at all") gave the music an often-breathtaking dimension. The songs waiting to be heard beyond the limited content of the Top 40 were exotic, seductive, challenging and constantly stretching the boundaries of contemporary popular music. In addition to the constantly growing and maturing new music of old standbys such as the Beatles, Stones, and Dylan, FM nurtured the creative output of dozens of individuals and groups that embraced the new rock.

Suddenly, rock was serious business. Its presence was being felt everywhere. Certainly in all of the media. Progressive rock stations sprang up all around the country. Serious journals of rock criticism, such as *Crawdaddy* and *Rolling Stone,* began publishing alongside the teen fan magazines. "Sit down and listen" rock concerts supplanted the record hops of yesteryear. The marriage of rock and cinema was consummated in films such as *The Graduate* and *Easy Rider,* as well as concert documentaries such as *Monterey Pop, Woodstock,* and *Gimme Shelter.* Even the

New York's
legendary
Fillmore East
showcased rock.

idea of rock festivals, which took as their models the jazz and folk festivals of the fifties and sixties, became commonplace.

Everywhere there was experimentation and high hopes for the future. Progressive rock exploded on many fronts during this period. One of the more colorful strains—literally and figuratively—was psychedelic rock. This late-sixties phenomenon attempted musically to replicate the mind-expanding effects of hallucinogenic drugs such as LSD and mescaline. The music incorporated feedback, loud amplification, synthesizers, Indian influences, and flashy, colorful light shows—all in an effort to recreate or enhance the sense disorientation of the drug experience. The psychedelic sound was also characterized by long improvisational jams and solos.

Psychedelic rock flourished on the airwaves and in the concert halls. The Fillmores East and West were twin meccas for it. Even the Top 40 charts were not immune—"Incense and Peppermints" by the Strawberry Alarm Clock made it all the way to the number one position. No group in rock 'n' roll escaped its influence. The Beatles were right there in the forefront with *Sgt. Pepper.* The Stones followed closely behind with *Their Satanic Majesties Request.* And so it went in all the major rock capitals around the world. But psychedelic rock is most closely linked to the city of San Francisco.

THE SAN FRANCISCO SOUND

The idea of a San Francisco Sound was more of a media creation than anything else. The music emanating from the City by the Bay was too diverse to be lumped together under any single label. Still, San Francisco was fertile territory for rock 'n' roll for several reasons. It was here that the West Coast version of progressive FM evolved under the watchful eyes and ears of the late Tom Donahue. Donahue was a former Top 40 disc jockey who became disenchanted with the limitations of that format, and inaugurated a looser "free-form" approach at a number of California FM stations.

San Francisco was also home base for promoter Bill Graham, who totally restructured the whole idea of a rock concert and how this music could and should be presented to large audiences. Instead of record hops or short performances by a large number of recording acts, Graham pioneered the presentation of lengthy performances by a couple of headliners in moderate-sized halls for a two- or three-day period.

San Francisco was also a natural gathering place for the more extreme elements of rock culture, who began to believe that, by virtue of their lifestyles, proclivities, and musical and sexual preferences, they were outcasts and outlaws. This group could be found in almost any major city in the United States (some minor ones, too), but their symbolic capital seemed to be San Francisco. They smoked marijuana. They experimented with LSD, more commonly referred to as acid. They lived in communes and took the idea of alternative lifestyles to radical extremes.

These were the so-called hippies and flower children of the sixties, and their chosen music was rock 'n' roll—not the three-chord variety of the fifties, or even the bouncy, reprocessed rock of the British Invasion, but a brand-new, sophisticated, complicated, technologically superior kind of music that came under the umbrella term "psychedelic rock." Although proponents of this music were generally gentle souls espousing a philosophy of love, peace, and happiness, they were perceived as outrageous, dangerous, and threatening to the more conservative elements of mainstream, status quo society. (Echoes of the reaction to early rock 'n' roll?)

The Jefferson Airplane/Starship

For all of the reasons outlined above, San Francisco became a natural spawning ground for psychedelic rock bands who either originated there or migrated from other parts of the country. In 1965 the Jefferson Airplane was the first San Francisco group signed to a major record label (RCA). By 1969 close to fifty bands from the area had recording contracts. But any list of memorable groups from the region must begin with the trailblazing Jefferson Airplane.

The Jefferson
Airplane:
Marty Balin,
Jorma Kaukonen,
Paul Kantner,
Grace Slick,
Spencer Dryden,
Jack Casady.

Formed in 1965 by former folksinger Marty Balin, the Airplane started out as a folk rock ensemble at Balin's club, the Matrix. The other original personnel included Paul Kantner, Jorma Kaukonen, Skip Spence, Bob Harvey (who was soon replaced by Jack Casady), and vocalist Signe Anderson. The group was signed by RCA and released their first album, *The Jefferson Airplane Takes Off*, in September 1966. Earlier that year, Signe Anderson left the group to have a baby and was replaced by Grace Slick, the lead singer of another very popular San Francisco band called the Great Society. Skip Spence also departed to form his own group and was succeeded by Spencer Dryden. This was the lineup that forged the Airplane's unique combination of folk, rock, jazz, pop, and blues. Their second album, *Surrealistic Pillow*, contained two Top 10 singles ("Somebody to Love" and "White Rabbit") and landed the Airplane squarely on the charts and in the hearts of rock fans the world over.

Over the next three years, the group produced an outstanding body of work and served as San Francisco's ambassadors to the world. *Rolling Stone's Illustrated History of Rock & Roll* described their sound in precise detail: "Balin's sobbing vibrato played off Slick's needle-sharp soprano, usually singing at the interval of a fifth: a folk harmony style that gives a hollow, austere sound unlike the sweet, 'close' harmony of singing in thirds. The rhythms had grown suppler and more powerful, and the guitars were stretching out in a bluesier, jazzier direction."

Although the music kept growing, the interpersonal relationships deteriorated. The group had more than its share of turmoil and tension. Personnel came and went with alarming frequency, and individual members occupied themselves with outside solo or duo projects.

In 1974, out of the ashes of the Airplane, Paul Kantner and Grace Slick formed the Jefferson Starship, and this new incarnation became successful in its own right, even scoring a couple of number one albums in the mid-seventies when Marty Balin joined the group for a while. But the same problems that plagued the Airplane resurfaced in the Starship, and by the end of the decade both Balin and Slick had departed for modestly successful solo careers.

Kantner persevered and put together yet another successful edition of the Jefferson Starship centered around the lead vocals of Mickey Thomas. By the mid-eighties, Kantner was gone, Slick was back, and the group name was shortened to Starship. Unbelievably, twenty years after the founding of the original Jefferson Airplane, the Starship scored their first number one single with a song that unabashedly pays tribute to their home base called "We Built This City (on Rock 'n' Roll)."

Big Brother and the Holding Company

Big Brother and the Holding Company formed in 1965 when Peter Albin, Sam Andrews, James Gurley, and David Getz began playing together at a series of indoor and outdoor jam sessions in the Haight-Ashbury section of San Francisco. But they were missing the essential ingredient that could accelerate them toward stardom—a dynamic lead vocalist. That problem was solved in June 1966 when a singer named Janis Joplin was chosen for the band.

Janis was born in Port Arthur, Texas, in 1943. In the early six-

Janis.

ties, she began singing folk, country, and blues music in bars and coffeehouses all around her home state. Lured to San Francisco by the flowering music scene there, she provided the missing element for Big Brother that ensured their success. They recorded their debut album for Mainstream Records in 1967, but it was their appearance at the Monterey International Pop Festival in June of that year that transformed them from a local sensation into a national phenomenon. At an event top-heavy with headline attractions and show-stopping performances, Janis clearly held her own in the company of rock giants such as Eric Burdon and the Animals, the Mamas and the Papas, and the Byrds. Based on that performance, the group's contract was bought out by Columbia Records, for whom they soon recorded the *Cheap Thrills* album. It went straight to number one and yielded the hit single "Piece of My Heart." Janis, together with Grace Slick, created an entirely new image for the women of rock 'n' roll. They were tough, hard-rocking mamas—a far cry from the girl groups of the early sixties.

Janis continued to mesmerize audiences. Trancelike, she screamed, contorted her face, pounded her feet, and commanded the stage with more urgency than any other woman in rock 'n' roll and most of the men as well! She was the best white blues singer of her time and her performances left critics raving and audiences clamoring for more. This type of adulation and singling out inevitably led to tension within the group, and Janis departed at the end of 1968 for a solo career. Big Brother continued for a while without much success, finally disbanding in 1972.

Janis persevered on her own, but she never really resolved the basic paradox of her life and career. She once summed it up quite accurately in a single sentence: "Onstage I make love to 25,000 people, then I go home alone." So intense was her need for love, so enormous were her physical and emotional appetites, that excess became the norm in her efforts to fill them.

She was found dead of a heroin overdose in a Hollywood hotel following a recording session for the *Pearl* album on October 4, 1970.

The Grateful Dead

One of the most amazing sojourns for any band in the history of rock 'n' roll was begun in San Francisco in 1965 by the Grateful Dead. Amazingly, it continues to this day. They have been an influential and consistent presence in rock 'n' roll for over twenty years now. The Grateful Dead aren't so much a band as they are a way of life. Their country, folk, blues, and rock mixture continues to have appeal to a wide cross-section of rock fans of many ages, but their main support comes from the so-called Dead Heads—the group's long-term, diehard fans, many of whom appear to lead otherwise reasonably normal lives apart from their obsession with this one particular rock 'n' roll band. Some of them follow the group on tour from city to city, swapping bootleg live recordings of their concerts with other Dead Heads, and constantly rehashing the group's past even as they push on into the future.

The Dead made a habit out of playing huge, free outdoor concerts in their native San Francisco and epitomized the drug-rock cultural connection of the time. They were signed by Warner Brothers Records in 1967. Their recorded work has always been spotty, with their live recordings usually among their best. But in the early seventies, the group produced two studio LPs that rank among rock's finest: *Workingman's Dead* and *American Beauty.*

Original member Ron "Pigpen" McKernan died in March 1973 from a liver disease related to heavy drinking. There have been personnel adjustments a couple of times since, but the basic

The Grateful Dead: Bill Kreutzmann, "Pigpen" McKernan, Jerry Garcia (foreground), Bob Weir, Mickey Hart, Phil Lesh.

performing unit of Jerry Garcia, Mickey Hart, Phil Lesh, Bill Kreutzmann, and Bob Weir remains intact.

The Dead have been involved in a number of rock 'n' roll landmarks: They were at Monterey, Woodstock, Altamont, and Watkins Glen. (The latter was the biggest single concert of the seventies, attracting some 600,000 fans to a speedway in upstate

New York to see the Allman Brothers, the Band, and the Grateful Dead.) They even played three nights at the Pyramids in Egypt in 1978.

At this writing, the group is an institution. Even their detractors have been forced to admit that, in the world of rock 'n' roll, where change is the only constant, there is something very comforting about the consistency, dependability, and longevity of the Grateful Dead. If I had to single out one reason for the group's intensely loyal following, it would be the uniqueness of each and every Grateful Dead live performance. Their music continues to rely heavily on spontaneity and improvisation. They have established such an intimacy and sense of community with their fans that each audience member can truly feel that any given concert is being done entirely for his or her benefit. It is that rare and most appreciated capability that continues to make the Grateful Dead one of the most special groups in the art and heart of rock 'n' roll.

The Steve Miller Band

Steve Miller was born in Milwaukee, Wisconsin, on October 5, 1943, and formed his first band, the Marksmen, at the age of twelve. He started a white soul group in college called the Ardells with Boz Scaggs and Ben Sidran. After a year of study abroad, he came back to the States and went to Chicago to absorb the rich blues influence of the region. In the process, he rubbed shoulders with the other hotshot white blues guitarists drawn to the scene, such as Elvin Bishop and Mike Bloomfield of the Paul Butterfield Blues Band.

In 1966 Miller moved to San Francisco, again lured by the

vibrant music scene. He formed the Steve Miller Band, which performed at many free outdoor shows and gained quite a following. They backed up Chuck Berry at the Fillmore West, and contributed three songs to the soundtrack of the motion picture *Revolution*. They appeared at Monterey and were offered a recording contract by Capitol Records.

Miller is rightfully credited with changing the business of rock 'n' roll in a couple of dramatic ways. First of all, he held out for a large advance ($50,000) to record his first album—larger than anyone else received up to that time. (Advances have escalated to stratospheric proportions since then for today's major rock stars.) Second, he demanded and received a higher royalty rate than was standard for even the most successful artists. And finally he insisted on absolute state-of-the-art technology for his records, thus achieving a cleaner, technically superior sound on his albums. These demands reshaped the relationship between artists and record companies for years to come.

The Steve Miller Band's first album, *Children of the Future*, was released in 1968 and included a side-long title suite that brilliantly synthesized all of the elements associated with psychedelic rock. Their second release later that year was the exquisite *Sailor* album, which contained the Top 20 single "Livin' in the U.S.A." Subsequent albums explored a variety of modes and genres. Miller has been accused of being a chameleon—adopting and discarding personas and trends in rapid succession. Problem is, he's a very good chameleon, mastering difficult and diverse styles as easily as most of us breathe.

In the mid-seventies, Miller's ear for the commercial really struck paydirt with a succession of Top 5 LPs such as *Book of*

Dreams and *Fly Like an Eagle*. Then he rolled right into the eighties with hit singles such as the number one "Abracadabra" (which was also a terrific video). Steve Miller is a self-confident individual who seems capable of commanding the attention of rock fans just about at will. He's been a performer for thirty years, a star for twenty, and a superstar for ten. He is a rare commodity in rock 'n' roll—one who seems capable of living his life and conducting his career strictly on his own terms.

Creedence Clearwater Revival

One of the most dynamic and successful bands to emerge from the San Francisco area, and yet have little to do with psychedelic rock per se was Creedence Clearwater Revival. Their sound was a much more basic, hard-driving style of rock 'n' roll that placed primitive rockabilly squarely into a progressive rock context with sensational results. John and Tom Fogerty were born in Berkeley, California, in 1945 and 1941, respectively. They met Stu Cook and Doug Clifford when they were in junior high school and began performing together as the Blue Velvets in 1959. They changed their name to the Golliwogs and were signed by Fantasy Records, where they enjoyed minor success, in San Francisco in 1964. In 1967, they changed their name to Creedence Clearwater Revival and adopted the bayou-flavored rock that made them famous.

From the start, Creedence juggled a number of seemingly incompatible elements and somehow, some way, made them work. They were simultaneously Top 40 and progressive. They were very singles-oriented, with hits such as "Proud Mary," "Bad Moon Rising," and "Travelin' Band." Yet they made collections that were eminently acceptable to album fanatics. They were the most commercially successful U.S. band from the late sixties into the seventies, yet they were embraced by that segment of the record-buying audience that abhorred commercialism.

For a while these inconsistencies didn't seem to matter, and Creedence rode the crest of big-time rock 'n' roll success. But inevitably the contradictions took their toll. Tom Fogerty left the band in 1971. They continued successfully as a trio for a year and a half, finally disbanding in October 1972. Each member has done solo projects or work with other groups, though never matching the success of Creedence. Then, in 1985, after years of seclusion and a long, drawn-out legal battle with his former record company over royalties, John Fogerty released a solo album called *Centerfield*. It shot to the top of the charts and yielded a couple of hit singles, proving conclusively that Creedence was no fluke of its time, and that Fogerty's brand of rock 'n' roll is as viable in the eighties as it was in the sixties and seventies.

Sly and the Family Stone

Sly and the Family Stone wrote one of the later, yet most influential, chapters of the West Coast music scene. Sylvester Stewart was born in Dallas, Texas, on March 15, 1944, and moved with his family to San Francisco in the fifties. He became immersed in music as a singer, guitarist, keyboard player, record producer, and disc jockey. Sly's influence came less from traditional centers of R&B and more from the progressive rock that surrounded him in his home city. In 1967 he formed the group that fulfilled his vision of combining black rhythms with psychedelic over-

Sly and
the Family Stone,
with Sly at the keyboards.

tones. Sly and the Family Stone put together a new musical combination of jazz, pop, soul, and rock that captivated audiences, black and white alike.

The group was interracial and intersexual, crossing barriers and breaking ground with each new record and live appearance. They began their assault on the American record charts in March of 1968 with "Dance to the Music," which peaked at number eight. Then, in January 1969, their irresistible anthem about brotherhood and racial harmony, "Everyday People," became number one on both the R&B and Top 40 charts. Their inclusion at Woodstock solidified and dramatized the crossover nature of their appeal as they delivered one of the most dynamic and memorable performances of the entire festival.

The band continued into the seventies with a string of hit albums and singles, but Sly's involvement with drugs and his resulting tendency to miss or arrive late for concerts and interviews inevitably led to the group's fall from favor and ultimate dissolution. Unfortunately, those problems continued into the eighties as Sly tried repeatedly and largely in vain to reclaim his place in the music hierarchy.

Santana

One of the last groups to emerge from the San Francisco area at the tail end of the sixties was Santana. Formed by and named after singer and lead guitarist Carlos Santana, the group built a solid following on the West Coast with their wonderful blend of hard rock and Latin rhythms that was totally fresh, original, and exciting. It earned them an invitation to Woodstock, where they nearly stole the show with a smoldering eight-minute version of

"Soul Sacrifice." Their debut album, *Santana*, was released in November 1969 and immediately went to number one.

Though the personnel changed regularly during the seventies, Santana continued to release sometimes groundbreaking, always-pleasing albums such as *Abraxas, Moonflower*, and *Inner Secrets*. Carlos became more and more fascinated with jazz-fusion music and began recording outside projects. In the eighties, Santana remains one of the more popular and innovative bands in rock 'n' roll with legitimate roots in the fertile soil of the San Francisco Sound of the sixties.

ERIC CLAPTON

Obviously, progressive rock was not limited to San Francisco, nor for that matter to America. Britain certainly had its share of adventurous and experimental musicians. Led by the increasingly progressive output of the Beatles, the Stones, the Kinks, and the Who, this second wave of the British Invasion included such innovative and creative groups as the Bee Gees (pre-disco), the Moody Blues, the Move, the Nice, Pink Floyd, Procol Harum, Traffic, and Jethro Tull. But the most influential new British group from mid-1966 to the end of 1968 was Cream—mainly due to the furor that surrounded their lead guitarist and sometime vocalist Eric Clapton.

This canonization of the guitar hero was nothing new. Right from the start, guitars were the primary instruments of rock 'n' roll. Surely the music could not exist without bass and drums, but the guitar has always been the fundamental symbol of rock—a symbol of its musicality, its power, and its sexuality. From Chuck Berry to Eddie Van Halen, the guitar hero is cen-

Rock guitar
virtuoso
Eric Clapton.

tral to the mystique and mythology of rock. And Eric Clapton is arguably one of the most gifted individuals to ever pick up the instrument.

He was born on March 30, 1945, in Ripley, England. He learned to play the guitar at the age of seventeen in 1962. A year later, he was part of one of the most highly regarded British Invasion bands, the Yardbirds. But so devoted to the blues was the young Clapton that, as the Yardbirds moved away from traditional blues and closer to a commercial sound, Clapton became disenchanted, left the group (to be replaced by still another great English guitar hero, Jeff Beck), and joined the more basic, roots-oriented Bluesbreakers, led by John Mayall. Then, in 1966, Clapton joined forces with Jack Bruce and Ginger Baker in the seminal progressive rock power trio Cream. The music world had never seen or heard anything quite like them—the loud volume, the great intensity, and the high level of musicianship displayed in lengthy free-form solos, jams, and improvisations. "Sunshine of Your Love" and "White Room" were their biggest hit singles, and all four of their albums made the British and American Top 40. Unfortunately, personality conflicts surfaced and Cream soured. They disbanded after a farewell concert in November 1968.

Just as volatile and even shorter lived was Clapton's next venture, the four-man Blind Faith, comprised of Clapton and Baker from Cream, Rick Grech from Family, and premier rock vocalist Steve Winwood from Traffic. The group lasted through one album and one tour before splintering in 1969. Part of Clapton's problem seemed to be an inability to reconcile his devotion to the purity and essence of blues guitar with the trappings of rock superstardom. He tried valiantly to shun the spotlight and recede into the background. He toured with the American duo Delaney and Bonnie. He played guitar on various projects with the Beatles, including George Harrison's "While My Guitar Gently Weeps" and John Lennon's *Live Peace in Toronto*.

Steve Winwood has kept rockin' through the sixties, seventies, and eighties.

In 1970 he recorded his first solo album, calling upon Leon Russell and Stephen Stills to help him out with it. For the first time in his career, he completely undertook the lead singer's role—with terrific results. He continued this dual role on his next project, the fabulously successful Derek and the Dominos, which included Eric as "Derek," along with Bobby Whitlock on keyboards, Carl Radle on bass, and Jim Gordon on drums, all former sidemen for Delaney and Bonnie. Their only studio recording was the phenomenal two-record set, *Layla and Other Assorted Love Songs*. Very few albums in rock 'n' roll deserve to be two-record sets. *Layla* is one of the exceptions. The album captured exhilarating state-of-the-art rock 'n' roll. Clapton's playing, augmented by the brilliant contributions of session guitarist Duane Allman, gave the record its distinctive, uncompromising edge. The group toured and delivered blistering live concert performances all through 1970 and 1971.

Regrettably, Clapton was in the throes of a life-and-death struggle with heroin addiction. He withdrew from public life for over a year to do battle with the problem. When it was under control, he attempted a comeback early in 1973 at the Rainbow Theater in London with the encouragement and assistance of friends like Pete Townshend of the Who, Ron Wood of the Faces, and Steve Winwood and Jim Capaldi of Traffic.

In 1974 he released the album *461 Ocean Boulevard*, which established the pattern for his recorded output since—more commercial, more relaxed, less intense, less driven. Since then he has recorded album after album of finely crafted songs and arrangements. He only tours when the mood or necessity strikes him. With this formula, he has no doubt alienated the blues purists in his audience, but, more importantly, he seems to have developed a medium of expression that he likes, that fulfills him, and that will hopefully keep him among us making music a lot longer than some of his more demon-dominated contemporaries who destroyed themselves with the "live fast, die young" philosophy.

JIMI HENDRIX

If Eric Clapton had an American counterpart in the sixties, it had to be the late Jimi Hendrix, who just about redefined the role of the rock guitarist in contemporary music. He was truly one of the most original, influential guitar masters of our time. He rewrote the book of rock 'n' roll guitar playing and slanted it to his own strengths, nuances, and eccentricities, which included fuzz tone, feedback, distortion, playing by hand, leg, foot, and mouth. Yes, it was chaotic, but in the chaos there was also fluidity, depth of emotion, range of expression, and more pure style per performance than ten other guitarists rolled into one.

Jimi was born in Seattle, Washington, on November 27, 1942. He learned to play guitar in his teens by listening to the great bluesmen and rock 'n' rollers of the time. After a stint in the Army, he moved to New York in 1964, where he backed up a variety of artists ranging from Sam Cooke, Jackie Wilson, and Little Richard to B. B. King, the Isley Brothers, and Ike and Tina Turner.

In the fall of 1966, Jimi went to England and put together the Jimi Hendrix Experience with Noel Redding on bass and Mitch Mitchell on drums. This was the trio that gave substance to Jimi's talent, creativity, and musical vision. They became the toast of London, but did not make their mark on the United States until an appearance at the Monterey International Pop Festival in June 1967. That performance, which was capped by Jimi's guitar-burning finale, catapulted him to superstar status.

Inner and outer tensions caused the Experience to fall apart in 1969, but Jimi never abandoned his quest for new sounds and new avenues of expression. He played at Woodstock, and later that year formed the short-lived Band of Gypsies with Buddy

Jimi.

Miles and Billy Cox. His last concert performance took place in August 1970 at the Isle of Wight. On September 18, 1970, he was found dead in a London apartment. He apparently choked while unconscious from some mixture of alcohol and barbiturates, becoming still another tragic casuality of the excesses of rock celebrity, and the unnecessary and often fatal connection between drugs and rock 'n' roll.

This romanticized notion of the media star who lives a short, dazzling life, then dies a horrifying, premature death is an unfortunate consequence of rock iconography. Of course, there is precedent for this scenario in every era and every medium of entertainment—Rudolph Valentino, James Dean, John Belushi—but rock seems to have the lion's share: airplane crashes, shootings, illnesses, auto accidents, suicides, but worst of all, purely self-destructive drug and/or alcohol abuse.

Many of these victims get elevated to a kind of rock saint-hood—some deserved, some not. The zenith of this kind of reverence just might be epitomized by the strange case of Jim Morrison of the Doors.

THE DOORS

The original Doors made their final concert appearance together in 1970. Their last new album was released in 1971. And Jim Morrison died in Paris under mysterious circumstances (though almost certainly drug- and alcohol-related) on July 3, 1971. Yet, as of this writing, the group's albums and repackages sell consistently well, a 1980 biography of Morrison called *No One Here Gets Out Alive* was an instant best-seller, the group's hits are radio staples, and someday there will probably be the film biography.

Only a handful of groups in rock 'n' roll history have consistently captured the imagination of each new generation of rock fans. The Doors are certainly one of them. This is surely explainable in part by the music. The songs and albums recorded by the group were exotic, mysterious, and richly textured. But the devotion accorded to the Doors goes beyond the music. It springs from the same source as the other most fascinating myths and legends of rock 'n' roll and is inextricably linked to the life and death of Jim Morrison

Jim Morrison was born on December 8, 1943, in Melbourne, Florida. His father was an admiral in the U.S. Navy. The two were, to put it mildly, estranged. Jim used to claim that his parents were dead. It is one of the great ironies of rock 'n' roll that, following Jim's death and the death of his wife Pamela two years later, control of the Morrison estate and any Doors-related properties reverted back to his parents.

Jim studied film at UCLA, where he met a classically trained keyboard player from Chicago named Ray Manzarek. One day in the summer of 1965, the two ran into one another on the beach in Venice, California, and worked out plans for the group that would eventually become the Doors (named after Aldous Huxley's book *The Doors of Perception*).

It has been said that in the summer of 1967 there were three absolutely essential albums: *Sgt. Pepper* by the Beatles, *Surrealistic Pillow* by the Jefferson Airplane, and the Doors' debut. I agree. *Pepper* was the ultimate concept album. *Pillow* helped to launch and define the San Francisco Sound. And the Doors? Well, the Doors were very special. That first album had something for everyone. It fulfilled all of the major requirements for

The Doors: Ray Manzarek, John Densmore, Robby Krieger, Jim Morrison.

great progressive rock of the time. The covers were inspired: Willie Dixon's "Back Door Man" and Kurt Weill's "Alabama Song." The originals were imaginative, sophisticated, and hypnotic, full of the tension, desperation, and psychodrama that imbued their best work—"Light My Fire" being the classic example.

On top of all that, there was Morrison himself—charismatic, maniacal, sexy, and totally self-destructive, a tendency that consumed him a little more than four years after the release of the Doors' first album.

So the impact of the group is partly explainable by the music, and partly explainable by the Morrison persona, frozen in time by his premature death. And maybe there is another element as well: the timeless way that art from one generation speaks directly to audiences of another generation. I asked Ray Manzarek about it in 1981. Here's what he said:

> *I think it's taken a while for a lot of people to understand the Doors, to put the Doors into some kind of historical perspective, and to realize the timeliness of the Doors, the universality of the Doors' message. You know, we didn't want to comment necessarily on what was going on; we wanted to talk about the human condition, about being alive. And I don't think anything has changed since the Doors recorded that first album in late 1966. I don't think the human condition for America has changed at all. I think the things we were talking about are just as pertinent, if not more pertinent, today: coming to grips with fear, coming to grips with reality, coming to grips with your own dark side, with the madness*

that lives within. You've got to conquer fear and you've got to conquer madness within you, or at least you've got to come to terms with it. Otherwise you're not going to be a whole human being. And that's what the Doors' message was all about.

In light of this, it's too bad Jim Morrison wasn't more successful at coming to grips with his own dark side.

Progressive rock was the perfect vehicle of expression for a generation that considered itself as forward thinking and special as this generation that came of age in the late sixties. They wanted nothing less than to change the world, overhaul its priorities, take over the power structure, infiltrate the mass media, undo conventional methods of conducting business and disassemble the military–industrial complex—all to the steady beat of rock 'n' roll. And as preposterous as these ambitions might seem now so many years removed from the era, these young men and women actually believed that these accomplishments were within their reach. No setback discouraged them. No disappointment altered their resolve. And they came together to celebrate their benign anarchy at every opportunity. New words like "be-in" and "love-in" were coined to describe these gatherings. And the rock concerts that went along with them just kept getting bigger and bigger, until . . .

WOODSTOCK

I'm a farmer. I don't know how to speak to twenty people at one time, let alone a crowd like this. This is the largest group of people ever assembled in one place. But I think that you people have proven something to the world—that a half a million kids can get together and have three days of fun and music, and have nothing but fun and music, and I God bless you for it!

—MAX YASGUR, the farmer who allowed his land in upstate New York to be used for the Woodstock Music and Art Festival in August 1969

Woodstock has already been mentioned a few times in these pages without any explanation or accompanying descriptive material, as if none was needed. Well, the time has come to attempt a brief interpretation. First, let me state the obvious. In the years since Woodstock, there have been many, many changes in music, in society, in people's ways of thinking about themselves and their relationship to one another and the planet. During that time, Woodstock has been chronicled, analyzed, dissected, plumbed for meaning, and pondered by a complete range of social critics. Recently, there has been a tendency to downplay Woodstock, make fun of it, minimize its importance. This is very unfortunate, because Woodstock was a truly remarkable event.

The festival was definitely the high-water mark for the sixties youth culture. Its combination of naïve political ideals and great rock music made believers out of the half-million actual participants, as well as countless others who attended vicariously, thanks to the various film, radio, television, record, magazine, and newspaper accounts of the event. It started out as a money-making venture—a rock concert, pure and simple, an attempt to duplicate or maybe even surpass the success of Monterey Pop, which attracted 50,000 people two years earlier. Three days in August 1969—the fifteenth, sixteenth, and seventeenth—were chosen by the promoters to present the finest folk and rock talent available, along with art exhibits and crafts fairs.

As local residents became fearful about the possibility of a hippie invasion, the location was changed from the village of Woodstock to the township of Wallkill, then finally to a farm at White Lake in the town of Bethel. The name, however, was retained. Everyone connected with the event was hopeful for a big success, but no one—absolutely no one—could have imagined the throngs it attracted, nor their accompanying depth of feeling about it all.

> *By the time we got to Woodstock,*
> *We were half a million strong.*
> *And everywhere there was song and celebration.*
> *And I dreamed I saw the bombers*
> *Riding shotgun in the sky*
> *And they were turning into butterflies*
> *Above our nation.*
>
> —JONI MITCHELL, "WOODSTOCK"

By all rights, it should have been a major disaster—the huge number of people, the rainstorms, the mud, the bad drugs, the insufficient food, the inadequate sanitary facilities—but it was not. Why did it work? What attracted so many people to such an event? Certainly the music had a great deal to do with it. What a lineup!

Among the acts scheduled to appear on Friday were: Joan

Baez; Arlo Guthrie; Tim Hardin; Richie Havens; the Incredible String Band; Melanie; and Ravi Shankar. On Saturday: Canned Heat; Country Joe and the Fish; Creedence Clearwater Revival; the Grateful Dead; Janis Joplin; Mountain; Santana; John Sebastian; Sha Na Na; Sly and the Family Stone; and the Who. On Sunday: the Band; Blood, Sweat, and Tears; Joe Cocker; Crosby, Stills, Nash and Young; Jimi Hendrix; the Jefferson Airplane; Ten Years After; and Johnny Winter.

Most of the artists were excellent. A few of them rose to the occasion and pushed themselves to deliver the performance of a lifetime. But there was more to it than just the music—much more.

Suddenly, in an instant, everything that had been bubbling beneath the surface of the sixties rock culture came boiling over onto the front pages of the nation's newspapers and across the screens of its ubiquitous television sets. All of the ideals of hippiedom, from the sublime to the ridiculous—long hair, love, peace, happiness, communal living, and rock 'n' roll—were all displayed on an international media clothesline for the whole world to see. And that was just the beginning. Still to come, in the spring of 1970, was a three-record set of highlights from the festival, and a three-hour motion picture documenting all facets of the event. The latter became a "how-to" manual for anyone who identified with the youth culture and wasn't there in the flesh, but wished they were.

If only for a moment, Woodstock definitely made the world sit up and take notice. All the evidence you need is right there in the film. If you've never seen it or haven't seen it lately, it's worth the effort to take a first or second look. The years have been kind to the musical performances. Many hold up extraordinarily well. Sly Stone, Alvin Lee of Ten Years After, and Santana come immediately to mind. The years have not been as kind, however, to the documentary aspects of the film. The trappings of hippiedom seem, at best, naïve and innocent, at worst, foolish and too self-indulgent to be taken seriously.

But the spirit of Woodstock still holds out a challenge to us all—the challenge of leaving the world a little better place than it was before you got here, and doing so not in isolation but in unity with your fellow humans. That challenge continues to surface and resurface at musical events from time to time, perhaps the grandest example being Live Aid in 1985. Joan Baez put it in perspective at JFK Stadium in Philadelphia when she opened the event by observing: "This is your Woodstock and it's long overdue."

That connection between eras, events and generations is absolutely essential to an understanding of rock 'n' roll, not just as entertainment but as a potent force for social change in all our lives. As long as there are consistent heartfelt attempts to meet that challenge head on, then Woodstock remains a vital and viable symbol and retains its status as an American culture landmark. And no amount of revisionist history is ever likely to alter that fact.

THE
SEVENTIES

The seventies began with such promise—amid such chaos. Vietnam raged on out of control, claiming American lives and dividing the nation, usually along generational lines. In fact, the gap separating young and old in this country was more like some unbridgeable chasm. Campus unrest continued unabated, perhaps reaching its zenith (or nadir) at Kent State University in May 1970. During a protest over the United States invasion of Cambodia, four students were killed when National Guardsmen fired into the crowd. Yet, through it all, rock 'n' roll remained the best barometer to measure the moods and attitudes of American young people.

The hottest groups at the beginning of the decade all had a couple of things in common. They were products of the so-called

Woodstock Nation, and many of them were plugged into world events and very active politically. The flavor of the period was best exemplified by the supergroup that was forged from three sixties institutions: the Byrds, the Buffalo Springfield, and the Hollies.

CROSBY, STILLS, AND NASH (AND SOMETIMES) YOUNG

Crosby, Stills, and Nash were an instant sensation right from the release of their debut album in the spring of 1969. Their sweet, exquisite harmonies belied the cutting edge of their best work. The songs of CSN (and Y) were multilayered and very personal. In one breath, they spoke of lost loves and wistful longings, while in the next breath, they pleaded the case for peaceful coexistence and environmental conservation.

There was an underlying seriousness of purpose about their greatest songs that galvanized audiences from coast to coast and instilled in them a tremendous sense of hope. When I asked Graham Nash about this phenomenon, he told me:

> *When you get a rock 'n' roll band that takes responsibility not only for its music but also for what it stands for, and what we stand for as people and human beings, and you put them together in the form that CSNY took, I can understand why people really enjoyed it. I thought it was particularly fine music, but it was music that had a deeper point, music that would initiate people into believing that they had individual power to change the world and should not have their future thrust down their throats.*

Neil Young, David Crosby, Graham Nash, and Stephen Stills—a supergroup whenever they choose to be one.

That was the spirit of the sixties in a nutshell. Unfortunately, it's a very difficult sentiment to live up to. And the group that best expressed it at the time fell apart and came back together again so many times that their leadership role dissipated. (CSN commented wryly on this aspect of their partnership in the 1982 hit "Wasted on the Way.")

Neil Young went on to one of the most eclectic solo careers in rock 'n' roll. Albums such as *After the Gold Rush*, *Harvest*, *Rust Never Sleeps*, and the recent *Landing on Water* contain some of the most adventurous and diverse music ever to be recorded by the same individual.

Crosby, Stills, and Nash survive into the eighties, but not without war wounds and battle scars. David Crosby's drug problems and bouts with the law are an ongoing tragedy. Stephen Stills's fluctuating weight and thinning hair are constant reminders of a generation's inevitable march toward middle age. Only Graham Nash seems impervious to the ravages of time. Physically and mentally, he projects an image of stability and elder statesmanship that is terribly attractive in a music littered with casualties. In fact, he and a handful of others, such as Paul McCartney, just might end up becoming role models for aging gracefully in rock 'n' roll—something that the music has been sorely lacking up to this point.

The success of CSN in 1970 gave every indication that the new decade would be a continuation of the old one, but there were clues early on that things were changing in the world of rock 'n' roll and changing for the worse. Bill Graham closed both the Fillmores in 1971, citing the rising costs of producing moderate-sized rock concerts and the extravagant demands of the rock stars themselves. But the worst blow to countercultural ideals occurred at the FM rock stations.

THE FALL OF PROGRESSIVE FM

Progressive FM was just about compromised out of existence. It became less and less rebellious as it became more and more successful. By the early seventies, with advertisers of every stripe clamoring to come on board, FM suddenly had more at stake. As a result, the stations toned down their revolutionary rhetoric and certainly lost some of their bite in the process.

Musically, the stations changed as well. Whereas the trademark of progressive FM had been that each deejay selected the music for his or her program, slowly but surely over the course of the decade this power was centralized in the hands of a music or program director, thus robbing the medium of some of its diversity. Ultimately, what had been progressive radio in the sixties was absorbed into a new umbrella format, known as album-oriented rock, or AOR. It's the homogenized, strictly formatted style of rock radio very common on the FM band of the eighties. Ironically, it often sounds like exactly the kind of radio that progressive FM was designed to serve as an alternative to back in 1967. Perhaps "regressive FM" is a good name for it.

Regardless of the changes in radio of the early seventies, or, for that matter, changes in society (the end of the war in Vietnam, Watergate, Nixon's resignation), the rock 'n' roll juggernaut just kept getting bigger and bigger. The cumulative effect of that bigness was fragmentation. Instead of any one single dominating force driving everything forward and rallying the mass audience, rock fans split up into dozens of different camps. Now, this is not to suggest that there weren't any discernible mass phenomena along the way. There always are and there always will be. As long as there are number one slots to fill on the singles and albums charts, there will be ambitious, talented performers striving to fill them.

Each year there were newborn superstars who took possession of the charts for greater or lesser periods of time, but no overriding, unifying force emerged in the seventies to match Elvis in the fifties or the Beatles in the sixties. Take Rod Stewart, for example. He began his career in the sixties as a vocalist with the Jeff Beck Group. In the seventies, he enjoyed double success as the lead singer of the Faces, and as a solo star with blockbuster albums such as *Every Picture Tells a Story, Never a Dull Moment,* and *A Night on the Town.* He came full circle in the eighties by reteaming with Jeff Beck on a wonderful version of "People Get Ready." Chicago is another band that never seriously rivaled the impact of the Beatles, but nonetheless enjoyed tremendous success throughout the seventies—and into the eighties—with their unique blend of jazz horns and rock 'n' roll on such hits as "Feeling Stronger Every Day" and "Saturday in the Park."

David Bowie is yet another superstar with roots in the sixties who came to prominence in the seventies as part of the short-lived "glitter rock" phenomenon. He enjoyed continuing success in the late seventies and on into the eighties by discarding the shock -rock theatrics and adopting a more sophisticated, mainstream persona.

• / / / •

ELTON JOHN

One of the biggest superstars of the early seventies was an unlikely candidate from England named Elton John. When his American debut was released in 1970, he was initially misperceived as a laid-back singer-songwriter because of soft ballads such as "Your Song" and "I Need You to Turn To." It wasn't until he began a series of live performances late in the year that Elton was recognized as a true rock 'n' roll maniac. With his garish costumes, outlandish eyeglasses, and dive-bomber stage theatrics, Elton soon proved to be one of the more outrageous and flamboyant rock stars of all time. But his onstage image was never a substitute for the quality of his music. Together with his lyricist, Bernie Taupin, Elton created a combination of ballads and rockers that stand side by side with some of rock 'n' roll's greatest. Number one singles such as "Crocodile Rock," "Bennie and the Jets," "Daniel," "Philadelphia Freedom," and "Island Girl," together with extraordinary albums such as *Madman Across the Water, Tumbleweed Connection, Good-bye Yellow Brick Road, Caribou,* and *Captain Fantastic and the Brown Dirt Cowboy* made Elton John the biggest solo rock star of the time.

He rode the crest of that intense kind of stardom for a couple of years in the mid-seventies, but by the decade's end even he was forced to settle for a lesser degree of success. Fortunately, he had a good perspective about it all, which he expressed in a 1980 interview:

> *I went through the period of being the big cheese. I enjoyed every minute of it. And things level off. It's a challenge if they don't level off. Your albums can't come*

Elton John—
outrageous in
the seventies,
still going
strong in the
eighties.

in the charts every week at number one. Your singles can't go gold all the time. But you have to sit down and say, "Hey, this isn't the reason I started doing this." I've always written for myself, no matter what misinterpretations have gone along the line with hit singles and things like that. You've still got to write for yourself and believe in yourself. And you can do no more than that. I'm just grateful to still be around after all these years, because what we did in six years up until 1976, what I went through, how many tours, how many albums I made—God, I should be in a loony bin by now!

One hopes that other shooting stars of the decade had as healthy an attitude about the fleeting nature of fame and life in the fast lane. There was Alice Cooper in 1972 and Grand Funk Railroad in 1974 and Peter Frampton in 1976 and the Bee Gees in 1978. Each one of them had their moment in the spotlight during the seventies. In retrospect, they relinquished it almost as quickly as they obtained it. Each of these groups and individuals made music that was as vastly different from one another as it was from the style and sensibility of the music that had defined the sixties. Cooper performed theatrical, glitter rock; Grand Funk epitomized American heavy metal; Frampton combined traditional hard rock with sensitive ballads; and the Bee Gees merged rock and disco. Given the wide range of styles to choose from, it's easier to describe the decade in terms of a series of phases or genres that attracted large and loyal followings.

In no particular order, the more noteworthy included:

HEAVY METAL

The late rock critic Lester Bangs once offered this thumbnail definition of heavy metal in *The Rolling Stone Illustrated History of Rock & Roll:* "Its noise is created by electric guitars, filtered through an array of warping devices from fuzz tone to wah-wah, cranked several decibels past the pain threshold, loud enough to rebound off the walls of the biggest arenas anywhere. Add the aural image of a battering ram, and you've got a pretty good picture of what heavy metal sounds like."

Ever since the late sixties and early seventies, heavy metal has been one of the most consistently popular forms of rock 'n' roll, particularly among teenage males. Each new generation of rock fans gravitates toward its own group of heavy metal practitioners. The term itself first surfaced in the William Burroughs novel *Naked Lunch*, and later showed up in the lyrics of Steppenwolf's 1968 hit "Born to Be Wild." It has become synonymous with the heavily amplified, thundering electric-guitar-dominated rock of bands ranging from Deep Purple to Def Leppard, from Black Sabbath to Van Halen.

But it all began in earnest with Led Zeppelin.

Led Zeppelin

Without question, the members of Led Zeppelin—Jimmy Page, Robert Plant, John Paul Jones, and John "Bonzo" Bonham— were the founding fathers of heavy metal. They set the standards by which all other groups who followed in their wake must be measured. And, even after all these years, most other bands fall slightly short of their mark. That's because Led Zeppelin transcended the genre and appealed to a wider audience than any purely heavy metal group ever could. Paradoxically, they managed to incorporate blues, folk, and jazz elements into a music that has come to denote guitar bashing, screaming vocals, and exaggerated posturing—with little else.

Led Zeppelin grew out of Jimmy Page's tenure with the legendary Yardbirds. When the latter group disbanded in 1968, Page joined forces with session bassist John Paul Jones to form the New Yardbirds. They enlisted John Bonham to play drums and Robert Plant to do lead vocals. The results were electrifying. They got their material together on a tour of Scandinavia in late 1968, then returned home to England to record their debut album. At this point, they changed their name to Led Zeppelin, reportedly at the suggestion of Keith Moon of the Who. The album was released in February 1969 and became instantly successful. Their second album came out before the end of the year and did even better. The group toured constantly in the beginning, solidifying their following. By the mid-seventies, they were the most commercially successful rock 'n' roll band in the world, topping the charts with album after album and breaking box office records—most of which had been set by the Beatles—in every country they played.

In 1975 Robert Plant was injured in an auto accident. This slowed down Led Zeppelin's output, but not their popularity. As often as they chose to tour or make an album, the fans turned out in droves to reaffirm their loyalty and fervor. Perhaps the key to understanding their huge success and tremendous appeal can be found in an analysis of their best-known anthem, "Stairway to Heaven," which many observers call *the* song of the seventies. It begins slowly, acoustically, ethereally. The vocal is soft and

Led Zeppelin
(clockwise from top
left): Jimmy
Page, Robert
Plant, John Bonham, John
Paul Jones.

dreamlike, the lyrics mystical and enigmatic. Slowly but surely over the course of its seven-minute-plus length, the track begins to build and intensify, gathering up steam and threatening to swallow everything in its path. Plant's vocal is now a desperate scream in a raging electric storm. Finally, the song climaxes in a cacophony of sound and fury that concludes with a plaintive, half-whispered, half-sung recitation of the song's title, leaving both performers and listeners alike exhausted and exhilarated. It is a rock 'n' roll masterpiece.

In September 1980, not long after the release of their album *In Through the Out Door*, John Bonham died of asphyxiation after consuming a massive quantity of alcohol. That December, Page, Plant, and Jones released a brief statement putting the group to rest as well. In the intervening years, Plant has embarked on a very successful solo career, and Page found a new outlet in a band called simply the Firm. At the Live Aid concert in 1985, there was an exciting emotional reunion of the surviving members of Led Zeppelin (with Tony Thompson and Phil Collins accompanying them on drums). There is also some talk of a new Led Zeppelin album and tour. Stay tuned for details.

On the heels of Led Zeppelin in the early seventies, there were a number of very successful English and American heavy metal bands, including Black Sabbath, Deep Purple, Judas Priest, Blue Oyster Cult, and Aerosmith. The form appears to be immune from trends and fickleness in the recording industry. No matter who or what is dominating radio airplay or the top of the charts, there are always heavy metal bands filling arenas and selling substantial numbers of albums. By the late seventies, it had become an international phenomenon with the huge popularity of Van Halen from America, Def Leppard and Iron Maiden from Britain, Krokus from Sweden, AC/DC from Australia, and Scorpions from Germany. Even more recent additions to the list are Ratt, Twisted Sister, and Mötley Crüe.

In October 1985 Jon Pareles of *The New York Times* offered this assessment of the function fulfilled by heavy metal:

> *What heavy metal bands unabashedly deliver is shock value—a taste of noisy, authority-threatening, vulgar thrills. They are an outlet for the feelings of rebellious adolescents. In that, they fulfill a function—public bad taste—that has always been served by some kind of popular culture, from bear-baiting to burlesque.*

MOTOWN REVISITED

Motown in the seventies was a far different record company than it was in the sixties. The label's most successful new act during that period was the Jackson Five, who continued the Motown tradition of number one singles. But the organization's tight-fisted control over its artists' careers and finances alienated some of Motown's most impressive talents. Many left the label by the middle of the decade. But even the sixties veterans who remained began recording very socially conscious material. The Temptations, for example, had hits with "Ball of Confusion (That's What the World Is Today)" in 1970 and "Papa Was a Rollin' Stone" in 1972, which were a far cry from "My Girl" and "The Way You Do the Things You Do."

Likewise, Marvin Gaye began writing fiery pleas about the

Marvin Gaye was a troubled musical genius.

war in Vietnam and the environment in his "What's Going On?" and "Mercy, Mercy Me (The Ecology)." By the mid-seventies, he began to explore a much more sensual kind of music with his album *Let's Get It On*. (The title song became a number one single.) His personal problems of divorce and bankruptcy plagued him for much of the rest of the decade, however, and into the eighties. Then, in 1982, Marvin left Motown for Columbia Records, where his very first album, *Midnight Love*, included the huge hit "Sexual Healing." His life and career seemed to be on an upswing when word came in April 1984 that he had been shot to death by his own father during a heated argument. A tragic end to the career of one of the most prolific, but troubled, stars of the Motown era.

On a brighter note, perhaps the most meaningful success for Motown in the seventies (and beyond) was reserved for the musical genius who began his phenomenal career at the age of thirteen with the number one single "Fingertips (Part II)" in 1963. Stevie Wonder followed that impressive debut with a succession of Top 10 records over the course of the rest of the decade. When he reached the age of twenty-one in 1971, he renegotiated his contract with Motown, taking creative control over his records. Then, in 1972, Wonder released the two albums that hinted at new directions and vistas for him. *Music of My Mind* and *Talking Book* contained music with a maturity and depth of expression unlike any he had previously recorded. He toured that summer as an opening act for the Rolling Stones, winning new fans with each appearance and broadening his appeal as both a singles and albums artist.

His next three albums, *Innervisions*, *Fulfillingness' First Finale*, and *Songs in the Key of Life* rank among the most honored and critically acclaimed records of all time. Following a brief slump in the late seventies, Stevie came back bigger and better than ever in the eighties with a string of hit singles and albums that continued to win accolades of every kind, including an Academy Award in 1985 for his song "I Just Called to Say I Love You" from the movie *The Woman in Red*.

Admittedly, his influence these days is more often felt in mainstream popular music than in rock 'n' roll. But, by any measure, Stevie Wonder is, artistically and commercially, one of the most important artists of our time. And, best of all, he's still at it with a vengeance. One can only speculate about the accomplishments that yet await him.

The great
Stevie Wonder.

PROGRESSIVE ROCK OF THE SEVENTIES

Progressive rock in the sixties encompassed a lot of territory: the folk rock of the Byrds; the jazz rock of Blood, Sweat, and Tears; the blues rock of the Electric Flag; and so on. It was a kaleidoscope of different styles, sounds, and techniques—all wrapped up directly or indirectly in the social ferment of the times. In the seventies, the phrase came to denote the slightly artier, classically influenced (critics would say pretentious) approach that was practiced by some of the biggest groups of the decade. The sound emphasized ornate orchestration and instrumentation. Contrary to the primitive directness and simplicity of basic rock 'n' roll, progressive rock was intricate, elaborate, and adventurous. It often took the form of lengthy suites or dramatic conceptual pieces centered around themes that were cosmic, spiritual, or grandiose.

The following were among the best:

The Electric Light Orchestra had a long string of intriguing concept albums, including *On the Third Day*, *Eldorado*, and *A New World Record*.

Emerson, Lake, and Palmer dominated the classically flavored progressive rock of the seventies with their albums *Welcome Back, My Friends, to the Show That Never Ends* and *Works: Volume 1* and *Volume 2*.

Genesis—not the pop-oriented Genesis of the eighties, but the theatrical, majestic Genesis of the seventies, found on albums such as *The Lamb Lies Down on Broadway, A Trick of the Tail*, and *And Then There Were Three*.

Jethro Tull may have started out the sixties as a folk-jazz-blues band, but by the early seventies evolved into a full-blown classical progressive rock group with their concept albums *Aqualung, Thick as a Brick,* and *Minstrel in the Gallery.*

King Crimson was one of the pioneer artistically oriented progressive rock bands with their 1969 release *In the Court of the Crimson King.*

The Moody Blues were also pioneers in the progressive rock genre as a result of their 1967 collaboration with the London Festival Orchestra, *Days of Future Passed.* Their recording of classically influenced concept albums continues successfully into the eighties—one of the few groups of their kind to have survived the changes of three decades.

Pink Floyd began experimenting with lengthy, spacey conceptual pieces as far back as 1967. But it wasn't until 1973 that they achieved rock 'n' roll immortality with the release of *The Dark Side of the Moon,* which sold over 4 million copies and stayed in the Top 100 pop album charts for over ten years, longer than any other album in music history.

Procol Harum, starting with their first single in 1967, "A Whiter Shade of Pale," until their breakup in 1977, explored a wide range of styles and sounds on their ten albums. Their most well-received progressive rock experiment was a 1971 live concert with the Edmonton Symphony Orchestra, released as *Live in Concert.*

Yes was one of the most successful progressive rock ensembles of the seventies. Their classically influenced albums, such as *Fragile, Close to the Edge,* and *Yessongs* parlayed great harmonies and extraordinary musical talent into phenomenally popular recordings. Yes broke up in 1980, but reformed in 1984 and scored a number one single with their song "Owner of a Lonely Heart."

Classy cosmic rockers— Pink Floyd: Nicky Mason, Dave Gilmour, Roger Waters, Rick Wright.

• / / / •

The Beatles must assume some responsibility for the rise of this kind of progressive rock—if only because it was their *Sgt. Pepper* album that hinted at the possibilities of a conceptual album and inspired numerous musicians to expand the narrowly defined boundaries of rock 'n' roll. Most of the major progressive

/ **153** •

rock groups of the seventies were British, but a few American bands, such as Kansas and Styx, also were very successful. The biggest and best of these bands made countless hit albums and toured the world relentlessly for most of the decade—probably unaware that, to some extent, they were primarily responsible for the "return to basics" revolution that exploded in the late seventies. Punk and New Wave were in large part a response to the ostentatious progressive rock that many critics felt had outlived its usefulness.

SINGER-SONGWRITERS

One major phase of early seventies music that was a natural outgrowth of the sixties was the singer-songwriter phenomenon. Taking their lead from Bob Dylan and his fellow songwriting poets, these writers and performers threatened to take permanent possession of the U.S. charts for a while. Their numbers included such great talents as Jackson Browne, Harry Chapin, Dan Fogelberg, Billy Joel, Gordon Lightfoot, Joni Mitchell, Randy Newman, Laura Nyro, Carly Simon, Paul Simon, and Cat Stevens, to name a few. Two of the most popular—one male and one female—whose success symbolizes the movement are James Taylor and Carole King.

We encountered the name Carole King earlier on. Her accomplishments as a writer in the sixties would assure her a place as one of the most influential women in rock 'n' roll history, but it doesn't just stop there. In the early seventies, after the end of her marriage to songwriting partner Gerry Goffin, Carole began a performing career that blossomed into one of the most successful of the decade. Her third release, *Tapestry,* captured the imagina-

Carole King is one of the most prolific and successful women in rock 'n' roll history.

tion of record buyers around the world. It was—and is—a wonderful album. There are terrific versions of two of her best songs from the sixties, "Will You Love Me Tomorrow?" and "(You Make Me Feel Like) A Natural Woman," plus moving ballads of lost love, found love, and friendship that truly strike a responsive chord. *Tapestry* stayed on the American album charts for an astonishing 302 weeks, making it one of the best-selling albums in the history of recorded music.

Many male performers came to prominence during the singer-songwriter explosion, but the biggest success of them all was a tall, shy young man from North Carolina (by way of Boston) named James Taylor. His very personal and heartfelt songs about love, friendship, family, and depression won him a wide listening audience. His second album, *Sweet Baby James,* reached the charts in 1970 and stayed there well into 1972. In March 1971, *Time* magazine put James on its cover as a symbol of the singer-songwriter phenomenon. His marriage to Carly Simon in November 1972 made them the reigning royal family of rock 'n' roll. (That union ended in divorce in 1982.) James's highly publicized struggle with drugs has taken the momentum out of his career on more than one occasion, but he's always managed to bounce back and reconnect with his audience, most recently in 1985 with a beautiful, life-affirming album entitled *That's Why I'm Here.*

At the end of the seventies, as radio playlists became increasingly restrictive and rock 'n' roll retreated to a more basic sound, the impact and visibility of the singer-songwriters lessened dramatically. Their material turned up only on soft rock or adult contemporary radio stations, and even then only the biggest hits by the biggest names. Thankfully, there are still a good many talented musicians choosing the form to express their art and touch all of our lives. You just have to look and listen a little bit harder these days to find them. But surely it is worth the effort.

SOUTHERN CALIFORNIA ROCK

Another very influential strain of rock in the seventies was centered around Los Angeles and Southern California. Certainly, it had its antecedents in the sixties L.A.-based bands, such as the Byrds and the Buffalo Springfield, but in the seventies a second generation of these musicians took on an identity and authority totally their own. At various times, this genre included Jackson Browne, Dan Fogelberg, Loggins and Messina, Poco, Linda Ronstadt, and J. D. Souther. Even Fleetwood Mac could be included on this list because, while it is true that they started out in the sixties as a British blues band, it wasn't until they relocated to California in 1974 and added American folk rockers Lindsey Buckingham and Stevie Nicks to their ranks that they became one of the top rock 'n' roll acts of the late seventies.

But the group that defined Southern California rock of the decade was the Eagles. Starting out as Linda Ronstadt's backup band, the original Eagles consisted of Don Henley, Glenn Frey, Bernie Leadon, and Randy Meisner. They very quickly established themselves as hitmakers in their own right with the release of their debut album in 1972. It contained three smash singles: "Take It Easy," "Witchy Woman," and "Peaceful Easy Feeling." Their basic sound was a skillful combination of hard-driving rock and sweet country harmonies. Though personnel varied, the hits remained consistent with singles such as "Best of My Love,"

"One of These Nights," "Lyin' Eyes," and "Take It to the Limit."

Then, in 1976, the release of *Hotel California* placed them at the pinnacle of rock 'n' roll stardom. It contained three more hit singles—the title song, "New Kid in Town," and "Life in the Fast Lane"—and sold 11 million copies. It took two years and a million dollars to make the followup, *The Long Run*. The group, which had faced tensions and problems almost from the very beginning, finally decided to call it a day in 1981. At this writing, Don Henley and Glenn Frey have established flourishing solo careers. But it was the Eagles as a group that left an indelible mark on rock 'n' roll. They were as important to an understanding of the Southern California lifestyle in the seventies as the Beach Boys were in the sixties.

SOUTHERN ROCK

As we've seen earlier, rock 'n' roll owes a great debt to the southern portion of the United States. There is a solid case to be made that it was born there, and virtually all of the great rock 'n' roll pioneers had roots in the South.

Southern rock took a dramatic turn in the late sixties and early seventies in the hands of a new breed of musicians—fiercely proud of their Southern heritage and thoroughly influenced by the complete range of progressive rock experimentation going on at the time. One of the prime movers of this new Southern Sound and sensibility was a former talent manager from Macon, Georgia, named Phil Walden. He started the small, independent Capricorn label in 1969, and the first group he signed was the Allman Brothers Band.

The Allman Brothers combined traditional Southern blues

The
Eagles—
Bernie Leadon, Don
Henley, Glenn Frey,
Don Felder,
Randy Meisner—
exemplified the Southern California
sound.

The Allman Brothers Band: Jai Johanny Johanson, Berry Oakley, Duane Allman, Butch Trucks, Gregg Allman, Dickey Betts.

and boogie with various rock styles, plus the added touch of jazz-like improvisations. The end result was a mesmerizing blend uniquely their own. With their twin lead guitars and double drums, the six-man Allman Brothers Band established the model that innumerable other groups followed. On the strength of their incredible live performances and a tremendous amount of FM airplay, they achieved mass popularity with the release of their third album, *The Allman Brothers Band Live at Fillmore East*, a two-record set.

Sadly, the group was plagued by tragedy. Guitarist Duane Allman was killed in a motorcycle accident in Macon in October 1971. Thirteen months later, bassist Berry Oakley was killed in an eerily similar accident just three blocks away from the scene of Duane's death. Dissension wreaked havoc within the group for the rest of the decade, causing them to split up and get back together again a couple of times. But, for all their problems and differences of opinion, musical or otherwise, the Allman Brothers Band made a lasting impression on the course of American rock 'n' roll, and opened the floodgates for a small army of Southern rockers who shared a common regional pride. The best of them were the Charlie Daniels Band, Lynyrd Skynyrd, the Marshall Tucker Band, the Outlaws, and .38 Special.

Rock steamrolled through the seventies. For most of the decade, it was business on a much larger scale than anyone previously imagined. To give you some idea of the scope of this success, the music industry spearheaded by rock in the seventies outdistanced all other entertainment organizations in gross revenues, including television, motion pictures, and professional sports.

The audience for rock 'n' roll had grown so large by 1976 that a new standard of measurement had to be devised to describe multimillion-selling albums. Gold records no longer accurately portrayed their accomplishment. So the platinum album award was created to honor albums that sold a million or more copies.

It seemed as if it would go on this way forever. But it didn't.

In the last few years of the decade, a number of events conspired to turn rock 'n' roll inside out and give it its biggest shakeup since the late-sixties rise of progressive rock. First of all, the disco craze swept the country. This smooth, slickly produced dance music just about took over American radio and the pop charts. In fact, the disco soundtrack album from the hit motion picture *Saturday Night Fever* became one of the best-selling LPs of all time. Disco was, at least in part, a reaction against the weighty, virtually nondanceable FM rock of the early seventies. Its enormous success angered and antagonized serious rock fans, who considered it mindless and superfluous. The arrival of the eighties signaled the beginning of the end of disco dominance. Although still around in one form or another, disco assumes a much less important role in popular music and looms as less of a threat to rock 'n' roll now than it did in the chaos of the late seventies. Why chaos? Because change inevitably breeds confusion, and change was certainly rampant in rock by 1977. In addition to disco, two other forces were at work that would alter the future course of rock 'n' roll: punk rock and a sagging economy.

PUNK ROCK/NEW WAVE

In the minds of many, rock of the seventies had become too massive, slick, and formularized, and, as a result, sterile, predictable, and, worst of all, *boring*. Some forms of progressive rock, for example, had become so top-heavy and bombastic that they seemed in grave danger of toppling under their own weight. The biggest rock stars operated like distant royalty. Affluence nurtured complacency and threatened to harden rock's arteries—a turn of events completely at odds with the best traditions and history of this rebellious *people's* music. Suddenly, unbelievably, rock had become the Establishment!

Fortunately, rock 'n' roll has a self-correcting mechanism that usually puts it back on track after it has strayed onto some wayward course. That mechanism came into operation in the late seventies, first in the form of punk rock, and then in its outgrowth, New Wave. Punk was, at its simplest, a militant retreat to rock 'n' roll basics. A primal scream for attention. A triumph of the visceral over the intellectual.

In England, punk was closely tied to the political and economic situation. Unemployed youth who genuinely felt that they had no future embraced punk rock as an outlet for their anger, frustration, and hopelessness. The most notorious early punk groups—the Sex Pistols, the Clash, and the Buzzcocks—clearly and uncompromisingly expressed those feelings.

In America, punk was always more strictly a reaction to the excesses of soulless, corporate rock. Initially, punk was resisted by American radio and the record industry as too negative, too unprofessional, too bizarre to be taken seriously. True to form, the music found outlets in small clubs, independent labels, and college radio stations—another example of recycling the path originally traveled by early rock in the fifties and progressive rock in the sixties.

Gradually, the music assumed a new identity and was gathered under the umbrella term New Wave, a phrase that basically connoted "acceptable" forms of punk rock. American record companies began signing and aggressively promoting groups such as Blondie, the Cars, and the Talking Heads. Similarly, such English New Wave acts as Elvis Costello or combined English–Americans—the Police and the Pretenders—gained strong footholds in the United States with music that was raw and hard-edged, but also accessible and ambitious. True to the original spirit of the music, New Wave kicked and screamed its way to a permanent place in the rock 'n' roll rainbow.

Another factor that changed the face of rock at the end of the seventies was the economic crunch that gripped the recording industry. Earlier in the decade during the oil crisis and corresponding economic woes, the record business seemed exempt from those problems. As we have noted, record sales and revenues just kept growing and growing. By the late seventies, however, reality caught up and the major labels began experiencing a slump. Grosses were off and industry spokesmen were pointing fingers and placing blame in a lot of different directions.

One of the most commonly heard complaints concerned the act of home taping. The practice of recording music with home taping devices is as old as the existence of those recording devices themselves. So it's hard to believe that home taping alone could have undermined the record industry to the extent that they claimed it did. Certainly, there were other factors, not the least of which were all the other leisure-time activities—video games, sports, and so on—competing for the young consumers' entertainment dollars. The record industry tightened its belt and introduced cost-cutting measures. These included elimination of many of the frills that had become associated with rock life in the seventies: lavish parties, unlimited limousine service, expensive promotional merchandise, and so on. Also, record company rosters were trimmed and fewer new acts were signed.

The glory days definitely appeared to be over, and rock 'n' roll began the eighties in turmoil.

THE
EIGHTIES

First, an explanation: Since the decade isn't over yet and since our ability to perceive current events is often very different than our perspective on history, this section is deliberately less inclusive and more speculative than previous ones. The eighties will be much easier to assess in about ten years or so.

Rock of the eighties has been as mercurial, energetic, and unpredictable as ever. The music continues to change and grow, to weather tragedy and adversity, to march confidently into the future—even as it looks back to its past for a sense of direction.

The economic problems of the recording industry were partially solved by an experiment that began on August 1, 1981. That was the day the twenty-four-hour, all-music video cable channel, MTV, debuted. Promotional films to support recording artists have been around in one form or another since the twenties and thirties, but MTV institutionalized the form, and in the process gave the record business a much needed shot in the arm. Industry sources cite MTV as the major new element in breaking new acts and stirring up flagging record sales.

FM rock radio still leaves a little something to be desired these days with its streamlined, homogenized formats. There are still too many national consultants who advise a number of radio stations across the country what to play and how to position themselves in their respective markets. These so called "radio doctors" tend to rob a station of local color and diversity. AOR (album-oriented rock) radio has also had to be on guard against competition from MTV and from the new incarnation of Top 40, called "Hot Hits," that swept the country in the early eighties.

As usual, the decade has spawned its own normal quota of superstars. There are brand-new ones, such as Prince and Madonna. And there are some old standbys who can still show the "kids" how it's done: Mick Jagger (with and without the Stones), Paul McCartney, Rod Stewart, Stevie Wonder, and so on. It has also been a decade of comebacks: James Brown, John Fogerty, Steve Winwood, Aretha Franklin, and Tina Turner, to name but a few.

Then there are those veterans who first became popular in the seventies, but really came into their own and are still going strong in the eighties. This wide-ranging category would have to include groups and individuals such as Dire Straits, Foreigner, Hall and Oates, Huey Lewis and the News, Billy Joel, Bob Seger, and Journey. This applies equally to women. Pat Benatar, Joan

Jett, and Ann and Nancy Wilson of Heart began their careers in the seventies, but they have virtually redefined the image of the hard-driving female rock star of the eighties.

There have also been some surprises. Familiar artists who

Tina Turner and Mick Jagger heat things up at Live Aid in 1985.

have "reinvented" themselves. That is, they completely dis-
carded their former identities, and consequently achieved even
greater stardom than they had previously enjoyed—David
Bowie, Phil Collins, Michael Jackson, and Kenny Loggins typify
this metamorphosis.

Finally, there are a couple of groups that began their careers
closely identified with New Wave, but have since emerged as
mass-audience superstars—Tom Petty and the Heartbreakers,
and the Police.

TOM PETTY AND THE HEARTBREAKERS

Tom Petty and the Heartbreakers' early releases got lumped in
with other New Wave albums of the seventies, but in reality Petty's musical vision owes more to the folk rock of the Byrds or the
Southern Rock of his hometown Gainesville, Florida, than it
does to anything else. His 1986 remake of the Byrds' "So You
Want to Be a Rock 'n' Roll Star" is ample proof of that. His
career was interrupted a couple of times by legal battles and
record company troubles, but by the beginning of the eighties, he
was routinely recording platinum albums and selling out concerts around the world. In 1985 the group backed up Bob Dylan
at the Farm Aid concert and subsequently went on tour together.
A perfect matchup of the sixties and the eighties.

THE POLICE

The success of the Police in particular illustrates how fast and
how far New Wave music has moved from its renegade origins to
major commercial acceptance. The group, consisting of Stewart
Copeland, Gordon Sumner ("Sting"), and Andy Summers

formed in England in 1977. Their early albums and publicity cast them squarely in the punk/New Wave mold, but their musical adventurousness and sophistication belied the punk or any other stereotype. Their sound was rich, textured, and eclectic, incorporating many interesting and diverse influences. By the early eighties, they were counted among the world's biggest record sellers, with platinum albums such as *Zenyatta Mondatta, Ghost in the Machine,* and *Synchronicity.* By 1985, each member had embarked on solo projects, the most successful of which was Sting's jazz-oriented and experimental *Dream of the Blue Turtle* album. They reunited for the 1986 Amnesty International tour.

The Amnesty International tour, which promoted awareness of human rights issues around the globe, was an example of one of the most heartening trends of the eighties. We have witnessed the return to a kind of politically aware, socially conscious rock that actually says something about the times in which we live and the problems we encounter at home and around the world. Of course, there were the Band Aid and U.S.A. for Africa recordings. In addition, we have groups such as U2 addressing the troubles between Catholics and Protestants in Northern Ireland. And individuals such as British rocker Bob Geldof organizing Live Aid, John Cougar Mellancamp getting involved in Farm Aid, and Steve VanZandt of Little Steven and the Disciples of Soul speaking out against apartheid in South Africa. These and other performers have begun to make a difference, once again taking their responsibilities as public figures seriously. It shows in the way they conduct their careers and personal lives. Let this be the trend without end.

The
Police—
Sting, Andy Summers,
Stewart Copeland—in an early
club appearance at New York's Bottom Line.

BRUCE SPRINGSTEEN

Perhaps the megasuccess of the eighties has been the story of that rock 'n' roll kid from Asbury Park, New Jersey: Bruce Springsteen.

FLASHBACK: It is the evening of August 14, 1975. I am sitting at a small table in the Bottom Line, one of the premier clubs to see and hear music in New York City. It holds a little over 400 people, and there's not a bad seat in the house. A sellout crowd is waiting eagerly for the early show to begin. The lights dim. A group of musicians scrambles in the semidarkness to find their places on the small stage. And finally an offstage voice intones: "Ladies and gentlemen, the Bottom Line is proud to present Columbia recording artist Bruce Springsteen and the E Street Band!"

The spotlight zooms in on a charismatic twenty-six-year-old wearing sneakers, jeans, a striped shirt, and a black leather jacket. He launches into a song called "Tenth Avenue Freezeout" and begins the mesmerizing, two-hour-plus concert that has been standing the world of rock 'n' roll on its ear. Springsteen is not a newcomer by any means. His performing career stretches back to the sixties. He released his first album, *Greetings from Asbury Park, N.J.*, in January 1973, and his second, *The Wild, the Innocent, and the E Street Shuffle*, before the end of that year. In the spring of 1974, rock critic Jon Landau described him in a review in *The Real Paper* with these famous words: "I have seen rock 'n' roll future and its name is Bruce Springsteen."

I remember my reactions to his first two albums very well. I was impressed with Springsteen's energy, enthusiasm, and writing ability, but overall the recordings struck me as disjointed and poorly produced. Meanwhile, the word-of-mouth about his live shows was phenomenal.

I hadn't seen Bruce prior to that night at the Bottom Line. That performance filled in the blanks and did for me what Bruce has done for countless millions since that night. It made us believers, witnesses to the greatest live show in rock 'n' roll.

At various times during the evening, just twenty feet or so from the stage, I saw glimpses in Bruce not only of great rock 'n' rollers like Elvis, but also some other media icons, such as Charlie Chaplin's "Little Tramp." There was also hilarious, comic story-telling, warmhearted camaraderie with the members of the E Street Band (particularly saxophonist Clarence Clemons), and an audience rapport that was unlike any I had previously experienced.

It was a great time to be discovering Bruce. In less than a month, his new album, *Born to Run,* would debut in the Top 10 of the album charts. Less than two months later, his face would simultaneously adorn the covers of both *Time* and *Newsweek* magazines. This latter occurrence probably hurt more than it helped. It smacked of hype and it angered and made as many people suspicious as it pleased. But it was just a matter of time before Bruce would prove his formidable worth.

FLASH FORWARD: It is the evening of August 20, 1984, nine years after that Bottom Line show. I am sitting with about 20,000 rabid, ecstatic Springsteen fans at the Brendan Byrne Arena in New Jersey on the closing night of Bruce's ten homecoming concerts. I came to the show with more than a few trepidations. How could Bruce, in a place the size of an airplane hangar, compete with my revered memories of the Bottom Line? Didn't something

Clarence Clemons onstage with the Boss—Bruce Springsteen.

have to be sacrificed in the growth from club act to arena phenomenon? Not to worry. There must be some law of physics to describe it: He fills whatever space he appears in—from living room to stadium. The crowd just basks in the glow of his magic. It's that great feeling you get when you spend some time in the company of someone special.

A lot has happened to Springsteen since 1975. A legal battle with his former manager put his career on hold for two and a half years. The album he released when it was over, *Darkness on the Edge of Town*, was full of the disillusionment and frustration of the experience. Somehow mass popularity eluded him until the release of his two-record set, *The River*, in 1980. A couple of hit singles and a world tour solidified his status as rock's reigning superstar.

In 1982 Bruce surprised just about everyone with a sparsely produced album called *Nebraska* that was more Woody Guthrie than Elvis Presley. With its stark portraits of the American landscape, most of them downbeat and tinged with despair, *Nebraska* proved conclusively that Bruce Springsteen was no ordinary rock 'n' roll star. And, also, that acoustic singer-songwriters still had their place in the eighties.

Then, in mid-1984, Bruce released the album that has so far defined the decade. *Born in the U.S.A.* has enjoyed the kind of success and acclaim reserved for only the most essential and influential records of the rock era. His cult following of the early seventies has grown to awesome proportions. He just may have the largest and most loyal audience of any pop star in any phase of the entertainment industry. The reasons are obvious. Bruce delivers an extraordinary one-two punch. The subjects he writes about—alienation, disillusionment, hope in the face of adversity—touch a deep and resonant chord in the hearts of his listeners. And he backs them up with live concerts that are the rock 'n' roll equivalent of "The Greatest Show on Earth." Also, there's no forgetting exactly how important a part of the show the E Street Band is: Roy Bittan (piano), Clarence Clemons (saxophone), Danny Federici (keyboards), Nils Lofgren (guitar), Patti Scialfa (vocals), Garry Tallent (bass), and Max Weinberg (drums). Guitarist and co-producer Steve VanZandt, Springsteen's longtime friend, left the band in 1982 for a solo career.

Bruce isn't just "rock 'n' roll future." On a good night, "The Boss" is the best of rock 'n' roll past and present as well. His instincts are unerringly on target. The stories he tells, the causes he espouses, the oldies he chooses to perform in his now three-hour-plus shows are exactly right.

There doesn't seem to be any question about it: Bruce is our Elvis or Beatles or Bob Dylan or anyone else he wants to be. If he has learned the harsh lessons of his rock 'n' roll predecessors, if his instincts as a writer and observer of contemporary life continue to serve him as well as they have up to this point, if his fervent belief in the healing spirit of rock 'n' roll continues undiminished, and finally, if he remains untainted and unaffected by the rewards of megasuccess, then I'm willing to bet that Bruce Springsteen will be playing an important role in the future course and direction of rock 'n' roll right into the twenty-first century.

Of course, rock 'n' roll's future is a very tricky subject to tackle. In the final analysis, *you*—the fan—are the ultimate authority on where this music is headed. It's your taste that counts. The albums you buy, the concerts you pay to see, and the radio stations you choose to listen to will really determine the future of rock 'n' roll. We've seen where it's been. Now it's up to you to decide where it's going and how it's going to get there.

ROCK
AND THE
MEDIA

The history of rock 'n' roll is so intertwined with radio—AM and FM—that it's best to incorporate that material into the chronological history of the music. But rock has had a unique impact on other electronic media as well, which will be explored in greater detail in this chapter.

ROCK AND TELEVISION

The relationship between rock 'n' roll and television has been long and stormy. They're like a couple of high-strung siblings who squabble and annoy each other all the time, yet deep down they need one another very much.

Both of these media powerhouses developed during roughly the same period of our history. The ability of television to create national sensations has existed from the very beginning of the medium. When Walt Disney did a miniseries about the life of frontiersman Davy Crockett in 1955, not only did coonskin caps become a national craze, but a version of "The Ballad of Davy Crockett" by Bill Hayes became a number one hit single. That should have been the definitive early clue about the intense cause-and-effect relationship that exists between television and popular music. There were others.

In 1956 Elvis Presley began a series of network television appearances on shows hosted by the Dorsey Brothers, Milton Berle, Steve Allen, and Ed Sullivan that produced extraordinary results. In a very brief period of time, those guest shots accelerated public awareness of his existence and uniqueness, legitimized his status as a pop culture phenomenon, and polarized audiences into camps of extreme like or dislike. The public outcry over his "suggestive" stage movements resulted in that infamous "waist-up only" appearance on "The Ed Sullivan Show." Needless to say, the republic survived.

Soon after the rise of rock 'n' roll, dance shows proliferated on local stations in major cities across the country. Usually hosted by hometown disc jockeys, these programs were low-budget affairs that featured high school students dancing to current hit records, plus occasional guest appearances by a recording star, who would more often than not mouth the words (lip-synch) to his or her latest hit—thereby avoiding the cost of musicians.

The most famous of these programs originated in Philadelphia and was called "Bandstand." It was hosted by a man named Bob Horn until 1956, when it was taken over by a former disc jockey from Mount Vernon, New York, named Dick Clark. The show was so popular that ABC Television decided to put it on the

Dick Clark (second from left) welcomes Dion (far right) and the Belmonts to "American Bandstand" in the late fifties.

network. It was renamed "American Bandstand" and premiered nationally on August 5, 1957.

Suddenly, rock 'n' roll had invaded our living rooms each weekday afternoon, sandwiched between a Johnny Carson–hosted quiz show and "The Mickey Mouse Club." Major stars clamored to be on to promote their latest records. The teenage dancers became national celebrities, attracting tons of fan mail each week. And Dick Clark laid the foundation for a media and financial empire that thrives to this very day. "American Bandstand" became a weekly show and moved to Los Angeles in the spring of 1964. It has weathered every change and trend in popular music and rock 'n' roll of the last thirty years. There have been other Dick Clark music shows—"The Saturday Night Beech-Nut Show" and "Where the Action Is," to name two—but "American Bandstand" is the one that has endured. Quite simply, it is an American pop cultural institution.

Another important development in the history of rock 'n' roll on television occurred on April 10, 1957. It was on that particular evening that the late Rick Nelson sang for the first time on his parents' television show, "The Adventures of Ozzie and Harriet." In an episode entitled *Ricky the Drummer,* the youngest member of the Nelson family sang a cover version of the Fats Domino hit "I'm Walkin'," which went on to sell a million copies. Furthermore, it launched Rick's career as a "teen idol," a term coined to describe him in a *Life* magazine article.

"Ozzie and Harriet" had been a welcome visitor in American homes since the heyday of network radio. It made a smooth transition to television in 1952. There were lots of family shows on the air, but America took special delight in observing the foibles of the Nelsons. That is why it was particularly significant that Ricky Nelson embraced rock 'n' roll. If Ricky could like this rebel music, then maybe it was okay for America's other sons and daughters to like it, too. Unlike Elvis, who was perceived as sexually aggressive and threatening, Ricky was clean-cut and safe. He brought prime-time rock 'n' roll into our homes on a weekly basis and did more to make this music respectable than any other early rocker. That is why his death in a plane crash on December 31, 1985, was particularly hard to deal with for those who grew up with him and followed the ups and downs of his career over three decades. Rick made the connection between television and rock 'n' roll perfectly clear. And it didn't take long for countless others to reap the rewards of that connection. But rock 'n' roll clearly owes a huge debt to the late Rick Nelson.

In the sixties, history repeated itself. When the Beatles made their first appearance on "The Ed Sullivan Show" on February 9, 1964, 73 million viewers fell hopelessly in love with them. Their phenomenal success had a number of reverberating effects on television. First of all, network programmers made room for prime-time rock shows such as "Shindig" and "Hullabaloo." Second, sitcoms and variety shows alike scampered to include rock stars in their plots and lineups. And, finally, an entire program was created to capitalize on the charm and success of the well-received Beatle movies.

MADNESS!! Auditions—Folk and Roll Musicians— Singers—Running parts for 4 insane boys, age 17–21.

That was the ad that ran in a show business trade paper called *Daily Variety* seeking actors and musicians for a new television series about a rock 'n' roll band. Two young enterprising producers were unashamedly attempting to cash in on the success of the Beatles. And it worked. Despite the calculating nature of it all, the Monkees were a smash. Within weeks of the premiere on September 12, 1966 of the show named for them, their albums and singles were topping the charts and making household names out of Mickey Dolenz, Davy Jones, Mike Nesmith, and Peter Tork.

Say what you will about how the group was put together; their music remains enjoyable and fun to listen to even today over twenty years later. Though the formula was borrowed from other sources, a case could be made that the Monkees were the first music video band—no small accomplishment in the context of the eighties. In fact, recent exposure of the Monkees on MTV has reignited interest in the group from a whole new generation.

There were a couple of variations on the success of the Monkees in the late sixties and early seventies, some live and some animated. The Partridge Family and the Archies, for example, had massive television exposure and corresponding success on the pop music charts. But the next major encounter between TV and rock 'n' roll came in the area of late-night programming. In the fall of 1972, ABC inaugurated a Friday night series in the 11:30 P.M. time period called "In Concert," which featured lengthy performances by rock's hottest attractions. NBC countered with "The Midnight Special," which enjoyed a healthy run from February 1973 to May 1981. A couple of syndicated series, such as "Don Kirshner's Rock Concert," also did well in this era.

The next development in the relationship between television

and rock 'n' roll came with the advent of widespread cable television programming and the debut of MTV—Music Television, the twenty-four-hour-a-day cable channel that shows nothing but rock videos (with occasional concerts and interviews).

Music videos are nothing new, of course. Any promotional film used to exploit music from the twenties to the eighties contained the seeds for MTV. But stringing them together into a nonstop barrage of our senses *is* brand-new and has had a dramatic impact on the nature of both television and rock music in the last few years.

As rock 'n' roll, MTV has had a major effect on the record business. How could it not? It is a national medium. A constant presence. Millions of subscribers on hundreds of cable systems are simultaneously exposed to new music and new recording artists every day. That's instant clout. MTV generated enormous record sales for many previously unknown groups that were not getting airplay on tightly formatted FM radio stations. (Duran Duran is a prime example.) And it created very distinctive and vivid personas even for established stars, such as Michael Jackson and ZZ Top.

As television, MTV is redefining the way we relate to the tube. In addition to its active role in all our lives, television has a passive role as well. It is environmental. It is a presence. It is a hypnotic, kinetic, ongoing experience. You don't actually watch MTV, you bathe in it. You let it wash over you. Sure, there's an occasional new video that you watch actively. If it's good enough, you might even watch it actively for a second, third, or fourth time. But after that, it becomes part of the landscape of the room—like the photo on the end table or the poster hanging on the wall. It is a very different way of watching television. MTV has also had a major impact on conventional network television, most notably in youth-oriented commercials, as well as the prime-time series "Miami Vice."

MTV is just the latest chapter in the ongoing alliance between TV and rock 'n' roll. And just as with Elvis on "The Ed Sullivan Show," there is a raging public debate between those who love it and those who think it is the end of Western civilization as we know it. Much of the controversy centers around the amount of sex and violence that shows up in a disproportionately high number of music videos.

Personally, I don't think we've sorted out what MTV means just yet, or what it will mean in the future. But, at the very least, I'm sure that the late Bill Haley would be pleased to know that his seminal fifties rock 'n' roll recording "Rock Around the Clock" has yet another new meaning for the eighties—and beyond.

ROCK AND THE MOVIES

Rock and the movies have always had a special relationship. This is partially due to the fact that it was a motion picture that helped to thrust rock 'n' roll into the national spotlight. "Rock Around the Clock," blaring out from the soundtrack of *The Blackboard Jungle* in 1955, sparked a revolution in entertainment. And the motion picture industry, ever vigilant against the inroads being made by its new competitor, television, seized the opportunity to exploit this new music and its brightest stars.

The first rock 'n' roll movies were hastily assembled affairs designed to capitalize on the popularity of this new fad. Bare-bones plots were devised to serve as an excuse to parade as many rock stars across the screen in ninety minutes as possible. The story lines may have been silly, but the moment the dialogue stopped and the music began, theatergoers sat up and took notice. In the Alan Freed movies alone, there are historic early rock performances by Chuck Berry, Bill Haley and the Comets, Little Richard, and a host of others.

Then there were the star vehicles. Whole films based around a single, charismatic rock 'n' roll star—Elvis Presley being the classic example. As far back as the late fifties and early sixties, the box-office value of a "teen idol" did not go unnoticed by the Hollywood establishment. For a while there, you couldn't go to a John Wayne movie without seeing a Rick Nelson, Frankie Avalon, or Fabian in the cast.

Rock films took a giant leap forward in the sixties with the Beatle movies. *A Hard Day's Night* and *Help!*, directed by Richard Lester, enjoyed the best of both worlds. They contained great rock 'n' roll, but they also worked on a purely cinematic level.

By the late sixties, rock soundtracks became a staple ingredient in conventional motion pictures as well. *The Graduate,* with music by Simon and Garfunkel, and *Easy Rider,* with a soundtrack full of rock classics, made rock 'n' roll an indispensable part of cinema vocabulary. *American Graffiti* is one movie where the music is just as important as what's seen on the screen. *The Big Chill* is another example.

It's gotten to the point where many of today's biggest hits are from the movies: Glenn Frey's "The Heat Is On" from *Beverly Hills Cop,* or John Parr's "Theme from St. Elmo's Fire." There have also been films based on songs or albums (Arlo Guthrie's "Alice's Restaurant" and the Who's *Tommy*). And even a couple of cases where the soundtrack from a movie did better financially than the movie itself. *FM*, for example, was a bomb at the box office, but its soundtrack LP, with music by Steely Dan and Linda Ronstadt, among others, sold millions of copies.

There are rock films of every conceivable variety: comedies, dramas, biographies, documentaries, performances, and so on. What I'd like to do now is put together a Top 10 list that is representative of the wide assortment of rock films that have been made in the last thirty years. Of course, it is a subjective list, but I have tried to choose movies that *say* something about the art of rock 'n' roll, the people who make it, and the people who love it. In chronological order, they are:

A Hard Day's Night (1964)
This is the one. The bona fide original. The best showcase for a brand-new rock 'n' roll phenomenon that has ever hit the silver screen. Of course, it helps that the music was terrific. But the group's rapport with the camera was absolutely delightful, and director Richard Lester's ability to capture the intensity and euphoria of Beatlemania was impeccable.

The T.A.M.I. Show (1965)
That's "Teenage Music International," a filmed account of a music awards presentation at the Santa Monica Civic Auditorium in California in 1964. This concert film was done at precisely that moment in our history when rock 'n' roll was in the midst of a total creative explosion. What we have here is a series

of one show-stopping performance after another by an honor roll of great talent, including the Beach Boys, Chuck Berry, James Brown, Marvin Gaye, the Miracles, the Rolling Stones, and the Supremes.

Monterey Pop (1968)
The Monterey International Pop Festival in June 1967 was the granddaddy of the rock 'n' roll music festivals of the sixties and seventies. All of the artifacts of that infamous Summer of Love are captured right here, along with top-notch performances by the progressive rock hierarchy: the Animals, the Mamas and the Papas, the Jefferson Airplane, and Simon and Garfunkel. Also, there's the Who's instrument-bashing finale, Janis Joplin's performance that got her signed to Columbia Records, and Jimi Hendrix's guitar-burning orgy.

Woodstock (1970)
For all the reasons mentioned earlier, this remains a "must see."

Gimme Shelter (1971)
Gimme Shelter is compelling cinema. How many movies start out to be pure entertainment and end up documenting an actual murder? How many films about rock 'n' roll that intend to illustrate its power end up instead capturing its dark side? *Gimme Shelter* is particularly effective when viewed as the flip side of Woodstock—a rock 'n' roll dream turned nightmare.

Let the Good Times Roll (1973)
This started out as a performance film of a rock 'n' roll revival

concert in the early seventies starring Chuck Berry, Little Richard, and Jerry Lee Lewis. By the time directors Sid Levin and Robert Abel got through adding interviews with the principals, vintage clips, and documentary footage, they ended up with a pretty solid chronicle of the early years of rock 'n' roll.

The Buddy Holly Story (1978)
It doesn't thrill me that this film played fast and loose with some of the historical facts, but it makes the list for three reasons: Buddy Holly's importance to the evolution of rock 'n' roll, the mythology and awareness of mortality that his death awoke in a generation, and the energy and intensity that Gary Busey brought to his Oscar-nominated title role.

The Last Waltz (1978)
Notice the timing here. Just as rock was entering a period of unparalleled change, along comes this film that serves as a fond farewell to a golden era. Initially intending to record the final performance by the Band in November 1976, filmmaker Martin Scorcese ended up documenting a loving tribute to all the ingredients of the rock 'n' roll stew. A wonderful movie.

The Kids Are Alright (1979)
Even though the Who carried on for a few years after the death of Keith Moon, and even though Pete Townshend and Roger Daltrey have continued their eventful careers, it became clearer and clearer each year that the Who really ended in September of 1978. With clips, interviews, and live performances, this film lovingly celebrates the band and its lofty place in rock 'n' roll his-

tory. This is how tribute films should be done.

This Is Spinal Tap (1983)
The only film of its kind on the list, this fictional send-up of heavy metal by Rob Reiner turns out to be much more than that as well. It makes wonderful fun of all of rock's excesses, pretensions, and stupidities. The performances are excellent and the observations about the world of radio and records are painfully on target. It is wickedly funny. One warning, though. The language and some of the situations earned this film its R rating.

A Note from the Author

Whew!

I feel we've been on a long journey together, from rock 'n' roll's early days, through its infancy, adolescence, and young adulthood. To quote the Grateful Dead, "What a long, strange trip it's been." Of course, the fallacy of an overview like this is that you can't cover it all, and you can't do justice to a lot of the things that you do cover. If I missed any of your favorites, I'm sorry.

For those of you who knew little about rock's past, I hope we have given you a starting place to find out more about it on your own. For those of you who did know something about previous rock history, I hope this book has helped to put it all in some kind of perspective.

Looking back on the project, I can honestly say that I really enjoyed re-examining my thirty-year association with rock 'n' roll. The best part was this: Whenever I got stuck searching for a word or phrase to describe some person or event in rock history, I would stop, go to my record collection, and play something appropriate. I can't begin to tell you what an inspiration and delight it was to be writing about the Everly Brothers while listening to their greatest hits, or thinking about Woodstock while listening to those classic performances. At every point in the book, this practice reminded me of exactly what it was about rock 'n' roll that made me fall in love with it in the first place.

Also, a wonderful coincidence took place on January 23, 1986. I was invited to attend the first annual induction ceremony for the brand-new Rock 'n' Roll Hall of Fame. It was a little incongruous at first—a black-tie dinner at the Waldorf Astoria—but by evening's end the spirit of rock 'n' roll had prevailed. What a remarkable array of legends and pioneers!

In alphabetical order:
- Chuck Berry was inducted by Keith Richards of the Rolling Stones.
- James Brown was inducted by Steve Winwood.
- Ray Charles was inducted by Quincy Jones.
- Sam Cooke was inducted by Herb Alpert.
- Fats Domino was inducted by Billy Joel.
- The Everly Brothers were inducted by Neil Young.
- Buddy Holly was inducted by John Fogerty.
- Little Richard was inducted by Roberta Flack.
- Jerry Lee Lewis was inducted by Hank Williams, Jr.
- Elvis Presley was inducted by Sean and Julian Lennon.

Keith Richards,
Chuck Berry, and
Neil Young jamming
away in New York at
the first annual
Rock 'n' Roll Hall of
Fame inductions.

As I sat there listening to the deeply felt and honestly expressed homages being paid to these rock 'n' roll heroes, I felt tremendously proud of having been a participant in this music from the very beginning right up to this awards dinner that brought it all full circle. During the spontaneous, all-star jam that capped the evening, I began wondering how I was going to communicate what all of this has meant to me in this book. Then, on the ride home that night, I realized that I am no less excited, amused, uplifted, entertained, and challenged by rock 'n' roll in 1986 than I was in 1956. I hope that all of you readers have the same good fortune thirty years hence.

Well, that's the story of rock 'n' roll up to this point. You see, if rock 'n' roll has proven anything at all since the days when pundits were predicting its imminent demise, it is that rock is an ongoing, everchanging story. In fact, even as I arrive at these final few words of this chronological history, someone, somewhere out there in somebody's basement or garage is already hard at work writing rock 'n' roll's next glorious chapter. I can hardly wait.

Bibliography

Betrock, Alan. *Girl Groups.* New York: Delilah, 1982.

Chapple, Steve, and Garofalo, Reebee. *Rock 'n' Roll Is Here to Pay.* Chicago: Nelson-Hall, 1977.

Clark, Dick, and Robinson, Richard. *Rock, Roll, and Remember.* New York: Thomas Y. Crowell Company, 1976.

Cott, Jonathan. *Dylan.* New York: Dolphin/Doubleday, 1984.

Davies, Hunter. *The Beatles.* New York: McGraw-Hill, 1968; revised edition, 1978.

Editors of Rolling Stone. *Rock Almanac.* New York: Rolling Stone/Collier, 1983.

Ehrenstein, David, and Reed, Bill. *Rock on Film*. New York: Delilah, 1982.

Fornatale, Peter, and Mills, Joshua E. *Radio in the Television Age*. New York: Overlook, 1980.

Friedman, Myra. *Buried Alive: The Biography of Janis Joplin*. New York: William Morrow and Co., 1973; New York: Bantam, 1974.

Gillett, Charlie. *The Sound of the City: The Rise of Rock and Roll*. New York: Outerbridge and Dienstfrey, 1970; New York: Dell, 1972; revised edition, Pantheon, 1984.

Hirshey, Gerri. *Nowhere to Run*. New York: Penguin, 1985.

Hopkins, Jerry. *Elvis*. New York: Simon and Schuster, 1971.

Hopkins, Jerry, and Sugerman, Daniel. *No One Here Gets Out Alive*. New York: Warner Books, 1980.

Marcus, Greil, ed. *Rock and Roll Will Stand*. Boston: Beacon Press, 1969.

Marsh, Dave. *Born to Run*. New York: Dolphin/Doubleday, 1979.

Marsh, Dave, with Swenson, John. *The Rolling Stone Record Guide*. New York: Rolling Stone/Random House, 1979.

Miller, Jim, ed. *The Rolling Stone Illustrated History of Rock & Roll*. New York: Rolling Stone/Random House, 1976; revised edition, 1980.

Milward, John. *The Beach Boys: Silver Anniversary.* New York: Doubleday/Dolphin, 1985.

Nite, Norm N. *Rock On: The Illustrated Encyclopedia of Rock'n' Roll.* New York: Thomas Y. Crowell Company, 1974.

Norman, Philip. *SHOUT! The Beatles in Their Generation.* New York: Fireside/Simon and Schuster, 1981.

Pareles, Jon, and Romanowski, Patricia, eds. *The Rolling Stone Encyclopedia of Rock & Roll.* New York: Rolling Stone/Summit/ Simon and Schuster, 1983.

Pollock, Bruce. *When the Music Mattered.* New York: Holt, Rinehart and Winston, 1983.

Santelli, Robert. *Aquarius Rising.* New York: Dell, 1980.

Scaduto, Anthony. *Bob Dylan.* New York: Grosset and Dunlap, 1971.

Schaffner, Nicholas. *The British Invasion.* New York: McGraw-Hill, 1982.

Whitburn, Joel. *The Billboard Book of Top 40 Hits.* New York: Billboard, 1983.

INDEX

References to
illustrations are in
italics.